"Does the hustle of the ho[...] right out of your Christmas? To[...] often a recipe for a yuletide dis[...] insel and give up altogether, gra[...] *g My Actual Christmas*. Alex Kuy[...] that will enable you to save your sanity as you savor the Savior, focusing on the true essence of the season."

Karen Ehman, Proverbs 31 Ministries speaker; *New York Times* bestselling author of *Keep It Shut* and *Listen, Love, Repeat*

"Do you love Jesus but secretly dread Christmas? This is the book you need in order to fall in love with the season again. While reading this book, I found myself regaining the same sense of wonder I had when I was a child on Christmas morning. Alexandra Kuykendall is like your personal Christmas elf. With humor, winsome stories, and practical ideas, she will help you put the happy back in your holidays."

Jennifer Dukes Lee, author of *The Happiness Dare*

"Alex's book is like a breath of fresh air. She shares real-life struggles we can all relate to. More than that, she provides practical help and inspiration to help busy moms just like me shape this season into one we can truly celebrate and enjoy. I highly recommend this book. In fact, it's going to be one of the first gifts I'll be buying and sharing this holiday season!"

Tricia Goyer, *USA Today* bestselling author of over sixty books, including *Where Treetops Glisten*

"Women give birth to Christmas. (*Pant, pant!*) Well, actually, one woman literally gave birth to the very first Christmas, and ever since, we women have been cocreating Christmas in our homes, families, and cultures. We long to remember the real reason for the season, celebrate it, and—here's a thought—enjoy it as well. But oh my, how to do so amid the mess of real life? Alexandra Kuykendall takes us on a quick trip to what matters most in her book *Loving My Actual Christmas*. In this short and practical read, she offers perspective and fun while also ladling out a healthy helping of *doable*."

Elisa Morgan, speaker; author of *The Beauty of Broken* and *Hello, Beauty Full*; cohost, Discover the Word; president emerita, MOPS International

"Slowing down in life is hard enough for women, but slowing down during the Christmas season seems to be the worst. Yet that's the time when there's so much joy, love, and peace to be celebrated within our homes with our actual, real-life people. Alexandra shows us how she took on the challenge of loving the Christmas season and how we can do that as well. As a mama of four, I know that there's nothing I want more than to love Christmastime with my family! Thanks for showing us how we too can take on this challenge!"

Jamie Ivey, host, *The Happy Hour with Jamie Ivey*;
author of *If You Only Knew*

"If you ever get the chance to read anything written by Alexandra Kuykendall, take it. She is a gentle, trustworthy storyteller who lives the words she writes about. In a noisy world, I deeply appreciate her thoughtful, grounded voice."

Emily P. Freeman, author of *Simply Tuesday*

"Of all the Christmas gifts you will receive this year, reading this book may be the most significant. Do you want a Christmas filled with memory-making rather than crazy-making? Do you want the holiday to be about the real rather than the artificial? Then join Alex in her four-week experiment to love (not stress about!) your actual Christmas. Using the pillars of traditional Advent—hope, love, joy, and peace—she offers the chance for meaning and contentment to replace hurry and frazzled."

Krista Gilbert, author of *Reclaiming Home*; cofounder, The Open
Door Sisterhood; cohost, *The Open Door Sisterhood* podcast

"I wish I had read this book eighteen years ago when our family began celebrating Christmas! Be freed from the chains of unrealistic expectations and soul-sucking busyness, while stepping into the beauty and life-giving force that is the celebration of Jesus's birth. Prepare to rethink your celebration and truly love your holiday this year."

Cherie Lowe, author of *Slaying the Debt Dragon: How
One Family Conquered Their Money Monster
and Found an Inspired Happily Every After*

"Alex had me laughing through the pain of identifying all too well with the expectations of a perfect Christmas. She reminds us to go easy on ourselves and those around us, offering gifts of hope, love, joy, and peace throughout the season."

Sarah Harmeyer, founder and chief people gatherer,
Neighbor's Table

Loving my Actual Christmas

AN EXPERIMENT IN RELISHING THE SEASON

ALEXANDRA KUYKENDALL

BakerBooks

a division of Baker Publishing Group
Grand Rapids, Michigan

© 2017 by Alexandra Kuykendall

Published by Baker Books
a division of Baker Publishing Group
PO Box 6287, Grand Rapids, MI 49516-6287
www.bakerbooks.com

Printed in the United States of America

Library of Congress Cataloging-in-Publication Data is on file at the Library of Congress, Washington, DC.

ISBN 978-0-8010-7536-0

The author is represented by Teresa Evenson of the William K. Jensen Literary Agency.

17 18 19 20 21 22 23   7 6 5 4 3 2 1

For Grandpa

We miss you this Christmas
and every Christmas to come.

Contents

Preface
A LETTER TO YOU

Dear Friend,

Oh how I suspect we may be living the same life, and so I call you "friend." You have picked up a book titled Loving My Actual Christmas, *and because of this I'm going to make a few assumptions. You are anticipating some hard in the upcoming holiday. Some stress. Some exhaustion. Some grief. You already know that your Christmas is going to have its bumps.*

Your anticipation of this likely stems from experience. A Christmas past was less than what you hoped for. Or there are new circumstances this time around that are going to make this particular year more difficult. Or maybe you recognize that you tend toward built-up expectations and subsequent disappointment, and so you want to be proactive and approach the season with some intentionality. Whatever the specifics of your motive, you hope to live in what "is," rather than what you wish for but is out of your control.

I am assuming we are alike in that yours is not a holiday filled with perfect gifts, impeccable decorations, and seamless relationships. That it is filled with constraints on time and money, and flawed people. That you are neither a model in an advertisement nor a 3-D walking Pinterest profile, but a real person. And you want to enjoy this Christmas. The one right in front of you. In the midst of all of the imperfect circumstances. You want to remember it as one filled with celebration and love, rather than frustration and regret.

This will not be a how-to-execute-the-most-seamless-epic-memory-for-your-family-ever kind of book. It will not tell you a formula for how to impress your mother-in-law or your neighbor down the street (you know the one—the front of her house was likely decorated by the Macy's Day Parade float designer with all of its inflatables and rotating lights). No, this will be about relishing what is in your life. Your family. Your budget. Your reality. You will be reading about my experiment in the context of my life. But my hope is you will experiment along with me. Perhaps duplicating what I try, but crafting your own experiment tailored to your actual Christmas.

My hope is you'll discover a bit of practical help and inspiration as you read these pages. You'll find some ideas you can implement to remove some stress, but it's more for your spirit to absorb the message of the holiday among the lights and gifts. I hope that you'll be reminded (or maybe learn for the first time) why we do this annual circus we call Christmas in the first place. That your heart will be refreshed as you let it linger a bit on the story where this all began.

As we remember the why behind the holiday, we shape what it looks like today. This year. In the context of our actual lives.

Your friend in the experiment,
Alex

Introduction

A RECALIBRATING OF THE SEASON

The Need

Every year I pull out my boxes of Christmas decorations from our garage attic and declare, "This year will be different!"

As I stand on the garage's concrete floor holding a mess of tangled Christmas lights, I wonder if I should toss the blob out and head to Target to buy new ones. But I'm too cheap and lazy to make the trek out in the Colorado cold. So as I unweave the strings from one another, I once again resolve when the season is done and it's time to pack up these lights, I will not throw them in the boxes in a tangled wad like I did the year before.

Those wads of lights represent how I feel at the end of the previous Christmas season. By the time I need to pack them up, I'm exhausted and done. I strip the decorations off the tree and front porch and stuff them in those boxes with a fury, figuring it will all get organized the following year. Because by the time Christmas has come and gone, I want nothing to do with the holiday.

This year already is different. We are coming off a difficult few months. In early October, my stepfather, Larry (aka Grandpa), passed away. He was a pillar in our family, a presence in our day-to-day, and our hearts are aching. In some ways we are going through the motions of life, through all the "firsts" without him. The first Thanksgiving, ballet recital, and now Christmas. It is new and it is hard.

By the time Christmas has come and gone, I want nothing to do with the holiday.

A few years ago, I walked through the maze of cubicles in my then office, making post-holiday small talk with my coworkers. Of course the standard question was, "How was your Christmas?" I was tired and frustrated to the point I couldn't even fake the rote, expected answer of "Great" or even "Fine." I was on the brink of quitting Christmas forever. "I hated it" I found myself repeating to my friends. "Other than the baby in the manger, I could do without the whole thing." Not exactly what I'd been aiming for in "the most wonderful time of the year."

My youngest was still a toddler. Normal life was already exhausting with four children, work deadlines, and sleep deprivation as the standard background music to my days. So on top of the usual stress and overcrowded schedule, I added in shopping, parties, special food, kids on school break (for nearly a month!), teacher gifts, family visiting, concerts, shows, church services, decorations, wrapping, and all of the million extra details that go into orchestrating Christmas. When it was over I wanted to collapse.

And yet I knew Christmas couldn't be avoided. In fact, it shouldn't be, because of that baby in the manger. That reason for the season. I knew the holiday itself was a good thing, just the way it was playing out in my life was crazy-making. How could I possibly do Christmas differently? So that I wasn't starting the New Year by ripping decorations off of the tree and slamming them into their boxes? There had to be a different approach. A better way.

But why all of this stress in the first place? Where is this coming from? Two things: 1. Expectations of the holidays. 2. Disappointment with the life that surrounds Christmas.

Let's talk first about expectations for those of us who are what I like to call "the orchestrators of Christmas." Just as Mary birthed Jesus on the first Christmas two millennia ago, we women rebirth Christmas every year with our efforts of putting on a production of special. We have standards of what we think Christmas should be. They come from our own childhoods, from commercials, from Pinterest. We consciously and unconsciously gobble up these ideas, most of which are based in beauty, fun, and general goodness, and digest them into our psyches, believing this must be how Christmas should be. The problem is, there aren't one or two special touches we connect with the season, there are a gazillion and one. And in our attempts to orchestrate them all, we overextend.

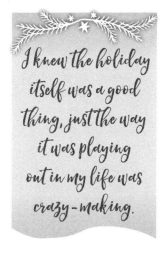

I knew the holiday itself was a good thing, just the way it was playing out in my life was crazy-making.

Then there's the life we're living, which offers the context for our Christmas. This holiday can act as an annual marker. As we end a calendar year we are reminded of where we are in life, which often highlights the places we wish were different or the people we miss. That empty seat at the dinner table can feel especially empty when it's Christmas dinner. It echoes back the loss from a strained relationship, death, or simply geographic distance. That life situation we thought this time last year would have changed for the better is still the same. A marriage struggle, an addiction, a financial hard place. No matter what the circumstance, this holiday marker can highlight the wound, reminding us that life is not as we'd hoped it would be.

The above two things combined is where the Christmas "whens" and "if onlys" come into play. They may run through our heads at a shouting volume or whisper to our spirits so slightly we barely notice they're there, but they impact us just the same. *When . . . we have a bigger budget, nicer house, better relationship with our extended family . . . then we'll have that perfect Christmas. If only . . . I could buy him what he wanted, I lived closer to my sister, didn't have an estranged relationship with my dad . . . then this would be a good year.* It doesn't matter what they are, we all have them. They can rob us of the joy of the season in front of us. Circumstances may not be what we want, but we can step over the "whens" and "if onlys" to notice God's gifts right in our midst.

So here we are at the front end of Christmas, and once again I am determining this year will be different. When I consider what I want to remember, or what I want my children to remember, a year from now, ten years from now, it's not an exhausted, over-whelmed, slightly crazed Christmas woman who is determined to make every moment magical and in the process gets angry and resentful. I know there must be a more sanity-infused way. One that involves not overdoing, but working toward relishing the here and now.

This experiment is being laid out in the context of my actual family right smack-dab in the middle of Denver, Colorado. I recognize many of my Christmas issues have to do with my time and place; in other words, there are a whole host of first-world problems involved in my holiday stress. This crazy I'm fighting against is part cultural and part self-imposed. And yet it is my actual life, and if I'm correct about my assessment of the women around me, I'm not alone. So I must face these first-world stressors if I want to enjoy this year with a bit of gratitude. I'm operating in a place of excess, dealing with the burdens of choice, abundance, and expectations.

And yes, my actual family, the people who live with me under the same roof, are part of the context as well. They are the ones for whom I feel some self-imposed pressure to create a magical, memorable experience. As far as a felt need for the experiment, this group both propels my desire to make Christmas special and my need to stay sane, so I can actually love the holiday with them. Let me introduce you to my household:

Derek

Age: solidly standing in his midforties

Favorite Christmas tradition: *Elf* (the movie)

On his Christmas wish list: children who sleep in past 5:30 on Christmas morning

Me

Age: three years behind Derek

Favorite Christmas tradition: Christmas Eve church service

On my Christmas wish list: new luggage (time to upgrade from the suitcases I've had since college that the practical in me just can't quit)

Gabi

Age: 14

Favorite Christmas tradition: gifts, both giving and receiving (it is her love language)[1]

On her Christmas wish list: makeup and clothes (she is 14, after all)

Genevieve

Age: 11

Favorite Christmas tradition: Christmas dinner with cousins

On her Christmas wish list: a buffalo hat, fur with horns, to wear to University of Colorado athletic events (Go Buffs!)

Gracelynn

Age: 7 (and starting to question the whole Santa thing)

Favorite Christmas tradition: decorating the tree

On her Christmas wish list: everything in the Target catalog (marketers know their stuff)

Giulianna (aka Lalo)

  Age: 5 (and still solidly in the Santa camp)

  Favorite Christmas tradition: decorating cookies

  On her Christmas wish list: a robotic dog that her sister
    pointed out in the Target catalog (guess who is now on
    my naughty list?)

I do not want this year to slip by, lost in the shuffle of the season's mayhem or clouded by my own disappointment of how things are different than I think they should be. This is the only Christmas my children will be the ages they are. Not to pile on the pressure, but I recognize this is a Christmas I won't get back. What do I want to remember a year from now, ten years from now, about this Christmas? It's up to me to do my part in making my answer a reality.

In order to prevent being in the same place next year, vowing this to be the year that is different, something must be done right here, right now within my own circumstances to enjoy the holiday in front of me. Because there must be joy in the chaos, hidden under the wrapping paper. A contentment set apart from spending and busy. There must be a way to savor what the season is truly about. It is here, in the middle of my actual circumstances and holiday, where I look for a new way to do Christmas.

The Experiment

If you read my book *Loving My Actual Life*,[2] you walked with me through an experiment. A trial-and-error kind of process, where I tested what would work in various areas of my daily routine to help me love my ordinary a little more. Part of what allowed me the space for this approach was time. I had no time constraints and so I chose a nine-month-long format for that experiment.

This Christmas experiment, however, is time sensitive. It is a given holiday season, a part of our calendar year marked out in weeks. Unlike what many retailers tell us, the season does not begin in July. Perhaps this is part of the reason we feel so much pressure to make it magical; it is time restricted and comes around but once a year. Because of this limited window, I will not be trying every tip I've ever heard about making Christmas work; I simply can't. (Truly, I might have a Pinterest-induced breakdown.) I will however be sharing some ideas I've gathered along the way, to act as a menu of small changes you can make to love this season a little more. You can find these practical tips in standalone sections at the end of the book, organized topically so you can figure out how your family will eat, or how you won't go bankrupt this holiday go around.

It is here, in the middle of my actual circumstances and holiday, where I look for a new way to do Christmas.

Though I won't be trying a million strategies, the experiment as a technique is not abandoned. I will be implementing an experiment of capturing the essence of the season. Well where do I find that? Target and Walmart would sure like to tell me where that essence is, on aisle 4 for $39.99. But truly? This is where I have to trust the church a bit. Not the people in the building where I go every Sunday, though I find that group to be quite trustworthy, but the body of believers in Jesus who have traveled the road of life through all circumstances the last two thousand years. There is a rhythm to the Christmas season that is found in the blueprint of the church calendar year known as the liturgical year.

Liturgy is simply the set order of worship. Sometimes this is at a single service, or in the case of the church calendar, over the course of the year. An order to what we celebrate when. As Joan Chittister says in her book *The Liturgical Year*, "Liturgical time raises our sights above the dailiness of life to the essence of life."[3] Um, yes please! I want to lift my eyes from the rolls of wrapping paper and stacks of Christmas cards to see the essence of this holiday, which is what this experiment is all about.

All of this to say I will use the church's themes of Advent, the four weeks leading up to Christmas Day, and then the season known as Christmastide (or more commonly the twelve days of Christmas), which celebrates Christmas not as a single day but as a stretch of time, as my starting place for the experiment. Just as candles are lit each Advent Sunday on an Advent wreath to represent hope, love, joy, and peace, I will delve into these themes each week as I experiment. These themes will guide my practical applications leading up to Christmas Day, with Christmastide carrying me into the new year, hopefully refreshed rather than exhausted.

Each week I will create a plan for how I will implement the theme, note what Scripture I'll be reading, share my attempts in carrying out the plan—highlighting the details of my own circumstances—and conclude with some thoughts on what I will continue, if anything, in future years. As you read along, you'll find some questions for reflection that may prompt you to consider how you could love your actual Christmas a little more.

Can I do this? Create an experiment where I'm able to savor the season in front of me without ending overwhelmed and bitter? Where I avoid needing a detox from the fa-la-la-la-la and the mistletoe? It is worth the try. Because hope, peace, joy, and love are certainly words I want to associate with this time of year. Rather than overspending, overeating, undersleeping, and underrejoicing, I want to notice the goodness God has offered in the here and now. In this year. This Christmas. Regardless of the circumstances. Because I don't want to resent this actual Christmas, I want to love it.

QUESTIONS FOR REFLECTION

1. What has been your Christmas experience in recent years? How do you feel knowing Christmas is approaching?

2. What would you like to remember about this Christmas season a year from now? Ten years from now?

3. What needs to happen for you to relish this season in front of you?

Words for My Actual Christmas

But the angel said to them, "Do not be afraid. I bring you good news that will cause great joy for all the people. Today in the town of David a Savior has been born to you; he is the Messiah, the Lord." (Luke 2:10–11)

ADVENT WEEK 1

Hope

Hope is being able to see that there is light despite all
of the darkness.

—Desmond Tutu

The Need

Hope. It is a word of anticipation, of belief that something good
is possible. It seems fitting to be in a place of hope as we enter this
Christmas season imagining that the good can happen. We know
hope is not a guarantee; otherwise it would be a contract. However,
hope believes that what we want can come true. It is a possibility.

This first week of Advent is centered on hope. In some churches,
the first Sunday in Advent is expressed as *expectation*, a word that
means "waiting with hope." Expectation reminds us of our hunger
and anticipation of a Messiah. I have been "expecting" four times
in my life and always the end result has been a swaddled bundle of

baby. We are familiar with expectation ending in the tiniest of new life. And each new life is born an embodiment of hope.

There seems to be a slight difference in these words *expectation* and *hope*. When I expect something I'm nearly certain it will arrive. When I hope for something there is less surety. My expectations around the season are tactical, what will happen where and when. My hopes go deeper to the heart of the matter. Perhaps expectations are how we want things to go down (great Christmas orchestrators that we are) and hopes are the desired lasting effects for relationships, memories, and growth.

I need to enter Advent, the weeks leading up to Christmas, with right-sized expectations.

My expectations are often loaded with longings I don't even know I have until I feel the disappointment creep in. What am I wanting? Perhaps I'm afraid to say because it feels unlikely. Like one of my girls who resists writing down the gift she truly wants for Christmas because she's afraid she'll be disappointed if it doesn't come. I wonder if I self-edit my true Christmas wish list as a means of self-preservation.

I must decide what my honest wishes for this Christmas season are. It seems like a good place to begin if I want to prevent that creeping disappointment. Maybe I need to enter Advent, the weeks leading up to Christmas, with right-sized expectations. On gifts. On relationships. On schedule. This may be the year of fewer packages under the tree, but plenty of memories cherished. It may be the year the Christmas concert isn't attended in order to have a Sunday afternoon to make some cookies . . . and enjoy the process. And the best way to get to right-sized expectations, to make some intentional decisions in my schedule, is to say out loud what I want.

When we peel back the layers of what we think we are hoping for, we discover what our heart truly desires—a relaxing season, a debt-free holiday, memories with those we live with or around. We can be honest with ourselves, at least, about what we are expecting, about what we are hoping for. And then we can make a plan and move forward.

But here's the messy part of the season: others have expectations too. Often they involve us, or at least our children, and all of those desires placed on our shoulders (orchestrators that we are) can feel like more than a little responsibility. They can feel like a pressure cooker about to explode.

We can't please everyone all of the time. A little bit of stating the obvious, I know. But even though we know something in our heads does not mean we always absorb it in our hearts. (Oh, this theme of expectation is thick and heavy.) We know it is humanly impossible to meet everyone's desires for Christmas morning or Christmas Eve, or the weeks leading up to December 25th, and yet we must face others' expectations. And we must be kind in the process. We must be respectful. We must figure out how to honor people's hopes in the best way we can while still sleeping more than two hours at a time and avoiding a holiday debt the size of a small nation's GNP.

The Experiment

How does one experiment with hope? How does one try to believe in something desired? It must begin with honesty. What do I truly want? When it's time to pack up the decorations, what do I hope we'll all remember? How do I hope I'll feel? My people will feel? What legacy will this Christmas carry forward?

Oh, this feels yucky and scary, because it could involve hearing what other people truly are hoping for too, and that can be overwhelming in light of what we've established: I won't be able to meet everyone's needs. But the way things have gone down in the past has left me pulled in a million directions, so I must face my heart and these conversations head-on. And now is the best time to have them, at the beginning of the season, rather than arguing about unmet expectations while driving to church on Christmas Eve (hypothetically speaking, of course).

So this week I'll do an inventory of what my hopes are for this Christmas, what those around me would both like and expect, and make a general plan to prioritize the elements that are most important to all of us.

Here it goes!

My Actual Approach

- Articulate (if for nothing else than my own benefit) my own expectations and hopes for the Christmas season and survey my people about theirs
- Draft a holiday schedule in light of said expectations
- Create a budget and a shopping list

What I Will Be Reading

Psalm 96

Matthew 1

SUNDAY

This actual life often doesn't prepare itself for Christmas the way I think it should. All of the details aren't in place in a way that is perfect, much less helpful.

Here we find ourselves in the first week of Advent, laying out the groundwork for what it means to be anticipating the birth of Jesus, and my family is coming off of a stomach bug that has swept through our house. Just as soon as the Thanksgiving turkey was blessed with prayers of gratitude, there were prayers for mercy in the midst of misery.

I am packing up ceramic pumpkins to make room on the mantel for the nativity. The gray November sky feels a bit forlorn. The weather and our mood. And yet . . . hope.

My hope is for the immediate and tangible—you know, my actual life: that those who are sick will recover and that the rest of us keep from getting it. I hope for space even though I can feel the muscles between my shoulder blades tighten because . . . Christmas cards. Their very possibility is one more scoop on the pile of expectations.

I am already finding this word, *expectation*, is a double-edged sword. One side conveys hope, and the other, holiday stress.

MONDAY

Okay, this might be a bit late in the game to be laying out expectations. People make plans a year, even years, in advance. The travel plans. The alternating families. The traditions that *always* happen. I recognize that making major shifts in our family's agenda may be difficult. That's not really my goal. I want to live within what is. Besides, now is better than four weeks from now. This is when the phrase "better late than never" is certainly true.

This is about uncovering hopes, mine and others', under a covering of grace.

What are people's actual expectations? Not the ones I've conjured in my head. Nor the ones they articulated four years ago and I haven't quite moved on from. This is about uncovering hopes, mine and others', under a covering of grace.

But this year things have been a bit upside-down for us. We are living in the reality of our actual family change this fall. Grandpa's absence is the bell that keeps ringing. Its reverberations, though sometimes quiet, are always present.

What do hope and expectation look like in light of loss? I hope to celebrate and yet I expect grief right there in the middle of it.

If Thanksgiving was any indication, grief will wash over me at the strangest of times. Flashbacks, memories, and anger taking their sudden swings to my gut. I'm not sure how to prepare for the unreliable emotions that will surely arrive.

I anticipate it will be hard on Christmas Eve when we are playing a game (the only night of the year we sit down as a family and play a board game). Grandpa's willingness to be silly with his grandchildren will be missed. I assume my mom will be lonely. That the extended Kuykendall family will get together as usual on Christmas evening. That our nuclear family decision around where and with whom and what times to do Christmas will be difficult. That's honest. And yucky. I'd rather avoid those realities and yet I know avoiding them won't make them disappear.

I figure the more specific I can be in what I want, the more likely I will be to reach my goal.

But I'm clinging to hope, the belief that something desired will come true. So here we are in the naming. I figure the more specific I can be in what I want, the more likely I will be to reach my goal.

Here is my grown-up Christmas wish list. This Christmas I hope to:

- Sleep. Simply put, I am more pleasant if I've slept.
- Give my children a few gifts they are excited to receive (and eliminate the extra fluff)
- Blast Christmas music
- Decorate the house so that it feels special, yet not overcrowded
- Execute it all in a way that implies to my family I'm grateful, rather than resentful, for this season with them
- Remember why we celebrate this holiday in the first place

So yes! I am going to hope that this year I can love my actual Christmas.

TUESDAY

Black Friday came and went. Not much shopping happened here other than the traditional Home Depot 99-cent poinsettias. (Disclaimer: This book is being written in 2016. I make no claims that the Home Depot in your area ever has, or ever will have, such a deal. But if they do, please get up at 7:00 a.m.—no need to be totally wacko with the 4:30 wakeup call—and drive to your closest HD and fill your car up with flowers. Because every person we have handed a red potted flower to this week has felt a little more special because of our efforts. The best dollar a woman can spend this holiday season.)

Cyber Monday was yesterday, and I avoided the temptation to browse. Partly because no time. And partly because I know myself. I get sucked in. *Oh look, 30 percent off of all books! I like books! Who doesn't like books? I'll buy books. Any books. Books for everyone!* . . . and, well, so it goes. I try to limit my online shopping to things that are already on my list. The whole impulse buy is now more dangerous for me with the click of a finger than the old-fashioned way of walking up to a counter holding my potential purchase. Amazon Prime has both made my Christmas easier and more dangerous in one fell swoop.

We need to get serious about this budget thing.

We probably should have tackled this subject weeks ago, but since our shopping is slow to get going this year, now will do (and a budget at any point in the game, no matter how late, is better than no budget at all—better late than never applies here too).

See: Taking It to the Bank, page 113.

And by "we" I mean the main breadwinner and me. I'm not a spender by nature. I like having a cushion in the savings account, and gift giving is my lowest of the five love languages, so

I don't expect this to be a battle of the wills or the spending habits. But we get back to that word *expectation*. What do I expect? What does he expect our credit card bill will look like in January? We can only know if we talk it through.

So today I asked. Not a big moment of a conversation, but we were alone and I was sweeping under the kitchen bar. It went something like this.

"What're you thinking about spending this year? You know, in January when the credit card bill comes, what would you be happy with as far as what we've spent on each other?" I figured our outside spending was pretty established. Extended family gifts have a set limit, we don't really exchange presents with friends, I know what I'll spend on teacher gifts. But our children? And each other? That's where we could go big or keep it simple. Where the discrepancies could play themselves out and the budget could be impacted in a significant way.

I can't ask about others' expectations and then be unwilling to hear their answers.

Derek threw out a number. I felt an instant internal pushback. (Remember my whole smug, "I'm not really a spender" thing? Perhaps pride was clouding my ability to self-evaluate.)

I started to do the math in my head. *This much for this child. And she wants a _____ which costs _____. And for this one _____. There's no way we'll be able to make that number work.*

"Really?" I kept sweeping. This could be a challenge. I was up to it. But I also knew there was some negotiating room.

"Well, you asked me." He could tell by my tone that we perhaps were on different planes. "That's what I'd be happy with."

Yes, all true. I can't ask about others' expectations and then be unwilling to hear their answers. I reached for the dustpan. We may have to come back to this.

WEDNESDAY

I'm a good candidate for a *Bless This Mess* cross-stitch on my wall or at least a magnet on my fridge. On top of the normal disorder, Christmas brings out boxes of more stuff. The wreaths, the garlands, the trees, the nativities. Where to put it all?

If I were a mediocre housekeeper who was on top of our standard chaos, I might look forward to decorating for the holiday, but because I'm already battling stuff management, bringing out more things to strew around the house creates tension in my neck. Though I'm not naturally organized, I still *prefer* to be organized.

So tonight when Genevieve asked if we could bring out the decorations, I did that mental calculating again.

Tomorrow we have gymnastics and indoor soccer.
Friday we're going up to Lindsay's to watch the football game.
Saturday Gabi has a birthday party.

And of course *everyone* must be present for the destruction of, I mean decoration of, the house. Anyway, my quick assessment was yes, this would be the best night of the next four to decorate.

Here is where mommy genius occasionally shows her head.

"On one condition: the house must be cleaned first." That was all the motivated elves needed.

With the Christmas carols going, I focused on the dishes in the sink, they focused on everything else. Within half an hour the living room, dining area, and kitchen were ready for the extras. Followed by a husband who got down the boxes from the garage attic after being asked only once, children who worked together to put the nativity on the mantel, and mini artificial trees assigned to girls' bedrooms.

And. Not. One. Argument.

Sometimes expectations are wrong. Sometimes things turn out better than this mama elf pictures. Sometimes we have a Christmas miracle.

Here is where this peeling back idea comes into play. I thought I wanted a decorated house. I thought I wanted help to make it happen, but what I truly appreciated was that we had fun together. We made a memory that may not be at the front of our brains forever but is woven into our experiences of life, and we got along. Truly my heart's hope was for us to love each other well. That is the reason this mama elf went to bed with a smile on her face.

THURSDAY

I'll confess the shine of one miraculous night does not last long. I feel weary. And not so much from the extra holiday madness, though I sense the creep that is happening, but life's weariness. I just spent an hour reading news stories, and worse, people's responses to them on Facebook.

I needed a break. Quiet. And no surprise, my night owl Genevieve was the last one up with me. It was time for a recalibration for me and a bedtime story for her. Back to the classic Christmas tale. I read out loud to her from Luke 2, in my personal favorite, *The Message* version of Scripture. I love that in this modern paraphrase, verses 8–20, which describe Jesus's arrival, are titled "An Event for Everyone."[1]

These shepherds, hanging out in their actual lives, most of them sleeping while a few got stuck with the night watch, weren't expecting the Messiah to come. At least not that night. Not in that way. It was an ordinary, every-night's-like-this kind of evening.

And then *bam*, the course of history was turned upside-down by God arriving as a baby. The angels showing up. And nothing was ever the same for them again.

That idea dangles in front of me. Nothing was ever the same for them again.

Nothing was ever the same for any of us. An event for everyone.

And yet I'm stressed about getting Christmas cards out. And that an acquaintance two times removed was snarky in her Facebook comment. And that my seven-year-old is determined to get a toy that I think is more expensive than any toy should ever be.•⋯⋯⋯

If this is the week of hope, I must hang my hope on none other than the trajectory of humanity changing when those angels showed up and woke the shepherds. Because nothing was ever the same again.

See: Reduce, Reuse, Recycle, page 116.

FRIDAY

Well, the conversations about expectations have been happening. I wish I could say it was because I was intentional, facing the potential discomfort head-on, but no, other people have brought up topics that needed to be covered.

I must hang my hope on none other than the trajectory of humanity changing when those angels showed up.

> "How do you see Christmas Eve going?"
>
> "If I ask for a new phone, I probably won't get one, right?"
>
> "When would be a good time for me to come over?"
>
> "What time do you think you all will get here on Christmas?"

I've been known to be an avoider. If the conversation is uncomfortable, I completely avoid it. And this year, just because of losing a person in our family, traditions and needs have shifted.

Once again, as these conversations have gone down, I'm reminded that my stress about them, about hurting someone's feelings, disappointing someone, is typically worse than the actual conversation.• We've talked through what we want and how this year might be different, and now we can all move forward into the rest of the season a bit more relaxed.

See: The Power of No Thank You, page 111.

So yes, I made progress today on the hard, but not to my credit.

SATURDAY

I'm teaching Sunday school tomorrow. Kindergarten Sunday school. No huge theological concepts to break down, only familiar verses for this middle-aged mom. Which is why I appreciate teaching these lessons: just like with my heart, I must peel back the layers and get to the central message.

Of course, right now in Advent, the stories center on baby Jesus. What kindergartner doesn't love a baby, right? But today's hero is Joseph. Truly he is a big hero, isn't he? That guy who had every reason to bolt and didn't. The faithful man who had a decision to make. Does he trust God's plans, or does he believe the whispers in his head that say this is just too crazy? Too out-there? Too embarrassing?

Talk about thwarted expectations. Mary is known for saying "I am the Lord's servant. . . . May your word to me be fulfilled."[2] So compliant it's almost unbelievable. Where's the anger? The disappointment? The feeling of "This is not how I planned it!" I guess Mary didn't have much of an option to change her circumstances. Joseph, on the other hand, did.

Perhaps he feels a bit more human to me in that regard. The dream. The doubts. The decision to stay.

As far as the original cast of characters goes, most did not have an actual Christmas that met their expectations. They of course did not know that their lives would become the biggest marketing strategy for the world someday, that Black Friday and ugly sweaters would stem from their nitty-gritty realities. They were just trying to be faithful in the face of fear, disappointment, and surprise. And they were filled with hope. That maybe if what they thought was happening was true, the world would be changed. Through this event, their layers of hopes and expectations are also peeled back and we see their hearts. Joseph was faithful in the midst of uncertainty because he believed God.

We are no different. We live in our actual situations knowing our hearts yearn for something bigger and more certain in an upside-down, fear-infused world. There is a reason we remember this story every year: because we need to. We need the reminder that pushing onward when plans change is sometimes the only way to move forward. Believing that there is a different ending from what is in front of us is *hope*. And like Joseph, our choice to believe in this greater hope despite circumstances that tell us otherwise is what defines our faith.

There is a reason we remember this story every year: because we need to.

Denial. Anger. Grief. All are realistic and understandable. But that balance between the ideal "perfect Christmas"—whatever that is in our imaginations—and reality has been going on since the baby in the manger. Because who knew God would arrive *that* way? Pretty sure Mary wasn't thinking a trough was the best bed for her precious newborn! If thwarted expectations are part of this year's Christmas, I guess I'm in good company. Mary, Joseph, the shepherds, and even the innkeeper were surprised by how that first Christmas unfolded. And God was present right in the middle of it. Emmanuel, God with us. What I hope for is bigger than the Christmas turkey or the cookie exchange. It is to join the first Christmas cast in their experience of Emmanuel; to get a taste of the shepherds' surprise, of Mary's wonder and Joseph's fortitude. It is to peer into the manger and find hope personified in the baby.

What I Learned

A week of focusing on what I hope for, what I expect, and what others expect of this season sets this year up with an honesty that is refreshing. Having these conversations—with myself, with others, and with

God—might not change the circumstances, but acknowledging the desires better prepares me for how to approach the holiday.

Hopefully this allows us to love each other to the best of our abilities within our constraints.

I feel better prepared to face the season with a true sense of anticipation when I have right-sized expectations. I have freedom to look for where God is working right here in the midst of my actual Christmas.

We were hardwired for hope by design. Our hearts yearn for the knowledge of God as a baby. Those first Christmas characters recognized this yearning as they encountered the physical manifestation of the holy. As my favorite Christmas carol, "O Holy Night," says so well, "Long lay the world in sin and error pining 'til He appeared and the soul felt its worth."

Emmanuel, God with us, was critical then and now. The famous lyrics continue, "A thrill of hope, the weary world rejoices."[3] There is something in me that is hopeful because only Hope himself can fill it, and he has arrived.

Practices I'll Continue

- Be honest with myself and others about my own expectations
- Ask others about their expectations for the season
- Create a budget as early as possible
- Read and reread the Christmas story

QUESTIONS FOR REFLECTION

1. What do you expect and hope for right now in your actual Christmas? How does it feel to say your hopes out loud?
2. What conversations need to happen to openly discuss expectations for the Christmas season?

3. Consider the original cast of characters in the Christmas story. How do their interrupted lives impact your perspective on this holiday and how you celebrate it?

Words for My Actual Christmas

Now faith is confidence in what we hope for and assurance about what we do not see. (Hebrews 11:1)

ADVENT WEEK 2

Love

Christmas, my child, is love in action.
Every time we love, every time we give, it's Christmas.

—Dale Evans

The Need

Here I am wanting to *love* my actual Christmas. To revel in the traditions. To celebrate the holiday. My mind starts going big and beautiful, equating loving Christmas with experiencing the best Christmas ever! You know, of the epic variety. But coming off a week of dealing with the reality of hope and expectation I recognize those feelings and thoughts and call them out. No, loving my *actual* Christmas has to do with celebrating in the midst of the grief or the tight budget or the circumstances I wouldn't hope for.

Love as a noun can be described as strong affection or liking, something that elicits enthusiasm, God's affection for humanity, and even a score of zero (tennis, anyone?).[1] If I am to hold love, this is what it would look like: affection, enthusiasm, and even a score of zero—as in, maybe I won't get much done on my to-do list. There's the whole "God is love" (1 John 4:8). He defines it. He holds it.

For God so loved the world . . . he sent a baby.

And the most famous Bible verse of all: "For God so loved the world that he gave his one and only Son, that whoever believes in him shall not perish but have eternal life" (John 3:16).

For God so loved the world . . . he sent a baby.

I know my babies were heaven sent. When I held them, cradled them and examined their toes, I knew I was experiencing the tangible miracle of new life. But this baby that changed the trajectory of humankind was different. He was God himself wrapped in the clothes of skin and bone. So it seems that love is key to the Christmas story. To the season.

And yet in the throes of the Christmas shopping, baking, driving, and general doing, my enthusiasm can get tarnished; the shine of Christmas can dim. My "strong affection or liking" for this whole holiday begins to disappear. People I *love* are all around me and driving me a bit crazy. If I am wanting to love my actual Christmas, I must examine what it means to have affection, enthusiasm, and a zero-sum game of productivity and make my decisions from there.

The Experiment

As I enter this week's experiment, I will take my cue for what love looks like in a tangible form from the various definitions my dictionary offers. To show affection to the people right in front of me. To experience a smidge of God's love for me. I want to be more focused on enjoying the season than getting the to-do list done.

But can I really when so much needs to happen that's dependent on me to execute it?

It seems there are actions I can take to love others and experience God's love that will push me toward loving this season as well. I do not want to resent what I cannot have. I want to focus on how God has shown me love through the gifts he has already provided. I resolve to celebrate what I am grateful for. To celebrate the

So it seems that love is key to the Christmas story.

very story, the Person, that is Christmas. My relationship with the baby in the manger is a love story that I can cling to. And when I do, I may just love all of the hoopla that surrounds this huge annual birthday party a little more too.

My Actual Approach

- Love the people around me through word and action
- Take daily inventory of what I am grateful for
- When given the choice between getting something done and enjoying the moment, I will take the moment

What I Will Be Reading

Isaiah 11:1–10
Luke 1:26–56

Sunday

Today was a day of parties.

Sunday school and Broncos on TV. A neighborhood bar and a magical Christmas gathering. Being together. A day of community.

My first party of the day was certainly church. We are *Celebration Community Church*. Everything about our name as a group of believers who congregate says joy for God's story in the world. And yet it is not a happy-clappy kind of church, where the smiles are plastered on as people pull in the parking lot. It's as honest a place as I know. Where grief and joy don't have to be separated. We live as best we can, fellow stumblers in the celebrating of God's love. So in a way, Sunday gatherings, church services, are a party. Whatever you call it, I know it's good.

And then a school party at a bar in the neighborhood. It was a fundraiser for a family in our circle with a son who has sudden and steep medical needs, and therefore, bills. Genevieve and I walked in to find the place filled to the brim with adults and kids rallying around a single family. Because this is love in action.

And, finally, the big hoorah for the day, one of our main family traditions: Mr. HUGS Christmas store. Technically it's a work party, because my husband's day job is to provide long-term affordable housing to those coming off of Denver's streets. He holds many hats in this small nonprofit ministry, Providence Network: raising money, supervising staff, communicating with the city, and being present. And that's what this party is about, being with people.

See: Saving Time for What's Most Important, page 105.

So we come together in real space and time during this busy season for a Christmas party of people gathering through generosity. Volunteers create a pop-up store that transforms a banquet room into a retail space of tables loaded with merchandise and a cashier to pay as you leave. Providence Network residents can shop for their families at a discount. Some people wrap gifts for the shoppers. Others serve chili and mac and cheese. Some are loving through setting up decorations, others by sitting and having conversation, and others in shopping for the special gifts for those who occupy their hearts. I cherish every bit of this celebration and am thrilled we get to be a part of this mingling of people. It is here, with kids tugging on my sleeve to get seconds on food or asking how long we are staying, that I stop and talk with friends.

Conversations cover upcoming moves, larger apartments, and new jobs. Kids being removed from their home and their mother's prayers for God to use the situation somehow. Memories of a father's last days on earth and a baby in the NICU. A microcosm of life in one evening. And all under the umbrella of a baby in the manger. An evening blocked out on our schedules to love others through presence.

Later, I laid my head on the pillow, grateful to have seen a glimpse of love in so many forms throughout my day. *Thank you, God, for this life. The big mess of it all and your presence in it.*

MONDAY

"How about we take the whole day off and go out to lunch?"

Genevieve was spending the morning visiting a middle school to see if it might be where she wanted to spend the following three years. I had a small window of time to take her to lunch, just the two of us. A rare moment in a family where everyone is clamoring for space and sound.

As an internal processor, I'm often not as present as I'd like to be. I must put the phone away, set the time aside, and pay attention to the girl right in front of me. Otherwise, I get caught up in my thoughts or, worse, my online space.

This season in all of its busy can distract me from my actual life.

Actively loving people has to do with capturing the moments that unexpectedly come up. Especially in a schedule that is already overbusy with all of the holiday extras that could put me at risk of missing the very people under my roof. This was a chance to stop. Look this middle child in the eye and ask her about her world, her hopes for school. Like any opportunity, I could take it or not.

Will those darn Christmas cards get done? Maybe not. Because I will choose to take this tween of mine to the mall and look for the new pants she needs. This season in all of its busy can distract me from my actual life. My people don't need the perfect Christmas, but a present mother, daughter, wife, friend.

Today I am grateful for:

Schooling options for my daughter
Healthy bodies and minds of my girls
A car that works to drive around the city
A little extra cash to buy my girl some new jeans
A job that allows for me to control my schedule

Zero-sum game = love.

TUESDAY

Love is not an unusual topic in the Christian faith. It's kind of central to it. So today, as I considered what it means to stand squarely in the middle of love, I scanned my house as if the answers might be somewhere right in my midst.

And wouldn't you know, as I walked by our coffee table full of books, this title caught my eye: *A Different Kind of Happiness: Discovering the Joy That Comes from Sacrificial Love.* Sacrificial love does sound like a different kind of happiness. Not easy. Maybe not even enjoyable. I picked the book up and opened it to find this:

Happily, Paul celebrated the truth that Jesus came into this world on a rescue mission that no Special Forces unit could ever pull off. He came to write a wonderful story that forgives us for telling a terribly bad story in which self-interest is featured. . . .

That same story of Jesus, Paul realized, empowers Jesus followers to tell a truly good story in which divine love, the kind that finds purpose and joy in sacrificing self-focused desires for the sake of another, expresses itself in even the worst of circumstances and relationships. And it energizes and sustains the storytelling expression of divine love by bringing into view the certain climax of eternal joy in loving community released in a perfect world.[2]

Love isn't always easy. It's not comfortable. It can be awkward. It is saying yes to an invitation when we'd rather not. It's adjusting our own Christmas plans to accommodate the hopes of another. It is not digging in our heels and wondering when we get to have Christmas our way. It's living a better story in front of other people that puts their needs first. This isn't about bad boundaries. This is about choosing to put someone else's expectations and hopes for this Christmas above our own. We are doing the choosing. It is active on our part, not passive. Because we are actively choosing, we then can't complain when things aren't comfortable or easy. We must take ownership for our decisions. My friend Sharon says the most important things in life require some sacrifice.

This living out our faith business is not for the faint of heart.

WEDNESDAY

Dang parenting anyway! It is the ultimate trial in loving, isn't it? The ultimate sacrificial I'll-lay-myself-down-and-let-you-stomp-on-my-heart-as-you-walk-toward-the-door-to-leave-me-someday kind of living.

Tonight was a night of arguing. Of negotiating. Of being the tough love in the house by saying, "You may not like me for making you do this, but because I love you I'm going to make you do it anyway." And in doing so, becoming the perceived enemy.

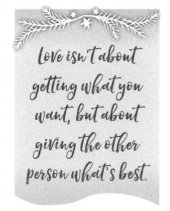

love isn't about getting what you want, but about giving the other person what's best.

Yep, parenting pretty much is showing love by setting limits. I haven't liked it when God has done that to me, and truly my kids don't like it when I offer the same kind of love. And yet I trust my children feel that the boundaries and the nos are a place of security. That love isn't about getting what you want, but about giving the other person what's best.

Dang parenting anyway! It can really put a damper on the Christmas spirit.

Today I am grateful for:

Children who have voices to speak
Food for my family
Freedom to parent as I determine
Freedom to celebrate Christmas

THURSDAY

It's been a cold few days in Denver, the coldest it's been in a few years. I woke up and reached for my phone: seven below zero. As I fell asleep last night I kept thinking of those who were falling asleep in the cold. Many were finding emergency shelter—more places are open in the city on record-breaking nights like these—but for some their shelter was cold. When it's below zero, lack of heat, of insulation, of proper clothing don't go unnoticed either.

And this is where gratitude comes in once again.

Thank you, Lord, for a warm place to sleep.
That my children are all snuggled in their beds.
That their tummies are full.
Thank you that we didn't fear for our safety last night.
That despite the parenting and marriage battles, we trust that
we truly love each other.
Thank you for utilities that work, money in the checking account,
and healthy bodies.
Oh Lord, I am grateful for this bed and time for sleep. Thank
you that my body does not ache from a hard day's work, and I pray
for those who are waking up this morning with muscles and feet
that throb from yesterday's labor. Comfort them.

On the topic of comfort, Lord, be with those who are cold this morning. Comfort them, Lord, and help them to know they are not forgotten by you. That you see them and love them . . .

And the prayers continued. One thing leads to another in this one-sided conversation. It's an opening of the heart where each whisper builds on top of the previous, to live in a posture of gratitude. And it is inevitable: when we express what we are grateful for, our hearts move toward those who are not in similar circumstances. Those who *are* cold. Those whose children *are* sick. Those who *are* hungry. And we petition God on their behalf.

If love is an action, it means showing up. My friend Krista said yesterday she was reading from 1 John and how it talks about "real love" as action.

This is how we know what real love is: Jesus gave his life for us. So we should give our lives for our brothers and sisters. Suppose someone has enough to live and sees a brother or sister in need, but does not help. Then God's love is not living in that person. My children, we should love people not only with words and talk, but by our actions and true caring. (1 John 3:16–18 NCV)

Yes, love is an action. It is Derek going to work every day to figure out how to make the numbers work. To pay the bills at Providence Network so women and their children leaving violence have a safe, warm place to live. So men who have decided rock bottom has finally arrived can find a place of support. It is my mom caring for my stepdad the years, months, days to the end. It is my neighbor getting up with her newborn in the middle of the night to feed and change and rock him back to sleep. It is the loyal love of Derek's parents evidenced by fifty years of the day in, day out of marriage.

Yes, maybe to love is both action and prayer.

Yes, love is an action.

It is also a prayer. It is the heart crying out to the one who holds the whole world in his hands. It is asking him for that next step of provision for someone else.

And perhaps the two are not to be separated, categorized in different camps: action vs. prayer. Perhaps action *is* prayer: through what we do is evidenced what we hope and want God to do in this world. And perhaps prayer is action, because we know that God considers the hopes and desires of his people, and therefore it's our most powerful avenue of change.

Yes, maybe to love is both action and prayer.

FRIDAY

A last-minute birthday lunch. Jen called to ask if I had time. Well of course not. I was speaking at a church downtown that morning on making the Christmas season meaningful and recording a podcast in the afternoon on keeping the holiday sacred. But there was an hour and a half window right there in the middle . . .

In the midst of all of this public talk of making the season count for something, was I willing to stop and pause to celebrate someone I love? The irony was blaring.

So though I didn't really have time, I could make time.

Late leaving the church, texting I was on my way, toting Giulianna with me from stop to stop, I finally rushed into the restaurant.

A wonder that four of us, Jen, Crystal, Kristi, and I, could have a coordinated window on a Friday afternoon, Kristi's actual birthday, to meet for lunch. Four of us with full-time or part-time work commitments, nine school schedules, and thirteen kids among us. I had to say yes. It was a miracle that it was even a possibility.

But this choice to love. To stop. To notice the people right in front of me. That is what this season is. It may have nothing to do with Christmas, a birthday, but it does have to do with the choice of making time. Zero-sum game as far as the Christmas tasks go. Winner = love.

SATURDAY

This morning we made gingerbread houses at my mom's. I held back the curse words while we tried to get premade sides of cookie homes to stick together with icing-paste. At one point Gabi chimed in, "This feels stressful." But once the construction was done and redone, with building codes broken all over the place, the gumdrops and peppermint decorations were nothing but fun.

And that afternoon as we started to wonder what was for dinner (because darn it anyway, everyone is still hungry when we have all this Christmas making to do), I decided a few sisters were getting on each other's nerves and needed a break from one another.

"Gracelynn, why don't we go do some Christmas shopping?" I suggested.

Each girl gets a chance to shop for the others in the family. With a budget provided by mom and dad and determined by their age. As a seven-year-old, Gracie had $7 to spend on each sister. From taco night to gifts on a shoestring, Walmart was about to meet all our needs.

As we drove the mile and a half from our house to the store, I asked Gracie what each person in our family might like. "Gabi would like a phone. Gugie likes puppies and iPads. La likes to snuggle." Nothing within her allotted budget, but oh how we learn about the limitations of Christmas early on. A starting point for some brainstorming and conversations around what people like and what we can afford, and of course the good news that hugs are always free to give.

As we wandered the aisles, Gracelynn's thoughtful nature showed through. Gift giving is my lowest of the five love languages. I tend to approach gifts with a tactical system. Lists. Purchase. Get it done. A check-it-off strategy so I can move on to more fun things, like baking and eating cookies. But Gracie is a gift giver. She thinks of the person, what they uniquely like, and watching her weigh her options among the Rollback prices reminded me why this tradition of giving gifts is part of our holiday. When done well, it shows love.

As we were walking to the checkout stand, the boxed Christmas cards caught my eye. HOPE inscribed across the front of the card. The O, a wreath with a baby in the manger in its center. Nothing else. And once again this weary soul rejoiced. It was beautiful and cheap, and exactly the kind of love note I wanted to send out to my favorite people this time of year. I dug through the mishmash of card boxes until I found a stack with this message across the front. I would make Christmas cards happen this year. Not because I had to, but because I wanted to do my part once again in reminding my fellow weary travelers on this earth that we celebrate hope wrapped as a baby.

I wanted to do my part once again in reminding my fellow weary travelers on this earth that we celebrate hope wrapped as a baby.

We left the store proud purchasers of a plastic cat, a hot sauce variety pack, some headbands, nail polish, and rhinestone broaches. Each item with its special recipient in mind, and within an hour of being home, specially wrapped and tagged by this gift-giving girl. And a stack of cards marked HOPE, which easily could have read LOVE, for Christmas is both.

What I Learned

Really, it's what I relearned. People require time. Relationships need our attention. Our physical proximity matters and eye contact makes a difference. Nothing earth shattering here. Simply to love others well, we must notice them and do what we can to meet their needs.

As far as the relearning, I'm remembering why we celebrate this story year after year. We must be reminded of God's love for us that came in flesh and bones and tears and emotions. A tangible love that could be rocked and swaddled, hugged and kissed. Our physical presence matters. In fact, God had to make himself known, his love known, by showing up in person (literally!). So no surprise that when we show up face-to-face, body-to-body, to love another soul in practical ways, our actions speak with a different kind of clarity.

What does this do to help us love our actual holiday more? We take our cues from Jesus and stop in the middle of the crowds and busy to notice someone right in our path. If he could make time for people, I can too no matter how many magical moments I'm trying to orchestrate. Sometimes that zero-sum game, that "I didn't get anything done on my to-do list," is worth it because the reward was saying yes to showing up on someone else's behalf.

If I can shift my priorities around enough to think of others' needs, true needs, in a way that reassures me I'm doing Christmas well—maybe even the way it is intended—I am that much closer to loving my actual Christmas season.

God's love for me is evident right here in the midst of my actual life. When I stop to notice the gifts he has already given me, the ways he has provided and met my needs, I don't have to search so desperately. My heart opens and the gratitude spills out. And out of that comes love. There is no better posture of my heart and attitude to love this holiday in front of me than with gratitude for what God has already done.

See: Saving Time for What's Most Important, page 105.

Practices I'll Continue

- Schedule my "main rocks" on my calendar as soon as I know about them
- Stop and listen to those around me in a way that is evident to them, through my eyes, my ears, and my body
- Build open spaces into my schedule so I'm available for an impromptu celebration

- Include sibling gift giving in our family's Christmas budget, and help each child make intentional purchases for siblings, cousins, and grandparents

QUESTIONS FOR REFLECTION

1. What if you made loving people a priority and got nothing else done on your to-do list this week? How would your stress level feel? How would your spirit feel?
2. Who might need some practical actions of love this holiday season right around you? How could you show this person or people a love that indicates you notice them?
3. How does the Christmas story remind us of how God's love meets our needs?

Words for My Actual Christmas

This is how we know what love is: Jesus Christ laid down his life for us. And we ought to lay down our lives for our brothers and sisters. (1 John 3:16)

ADVENT WEEK 3

Joy

Joy is the serious business of Heaven.

—C. S. Lewis

The Need

When I hear the word *joy* this time of year, I hear "Joy to the world, the Lord has come"[1] start to play in my head. This familiar Christmas carol is not the quiet, contemplative, tender tune of "Silent Night." Nor is it the holy and reverent "O Holy Night." This is the one where the horns come out. Where you almost shout the words because it is a declaration, a proclamation, a telling all who can hear that something has just happened.

But are we approaching this season like a party in the streets? Like a celebration full of laughter? Perhaps the stress of the extra spending or schedule, or maybe the circumstances of what this Christmas looks like in comparison to our conjured-up expectations, is getting in our way. And yet if we are not naturally full of joy, the emphatic, deep-in-our-hearts delight that Christmas is here, maybe it is something we must work toward.

Because if the aim is to love my actual Christmas, the one this year that I'm smack in the middle of, joy must be part of it, right? If there's no joy, then what's the point? We decide to have a miserable holiday? Well, that's certainly an option, but then loving it wouldn't really be our aim, would it?

First, I must examine my understanding of this word *joy*. This word that is often interchanged with *happy*. Happiness is based on temporary circumstances, we like to say. It comes and goes with the moment. But joy, that settling-in-the-spirit kind of happiness, is found in a deeper place. In church circles we point to Jesus to offer that underlying foundation. So, is it possible to be sad and joyful all at once? How does one intentionally add joy to a season that may feel painful? Can I simply decide to be joyful? I hope to find out.

The Experiment

I will be building on the two previous weeks' experiments. If my expectations were determined a few weeks ago, I must deal with how they bump up against the "actual Christmas" this week. I know I can't force feelings to come on their own, but I can certainly do my part to create an environment that works toward them and do my best to set the table figuratively for joy, and literally for people to gather and celebrate. I can build in celebration with an intentional twist not because of, but in spite of, circumstances.

The fact that this week follows *love* is fitting. In the book of John, Jesus tells his disciples to remain in his love and to love one another. Sandwiched between those two commands he says, "I have told you this so that my joy may be in you and that your joy may be complete" (John 15:11). It turns out joy is centered in accepting God's love and then turning around and loving others. In this context of giving and receiving love, joy is grown.

Jesus continues, "Very truly I tell you, you will weep and mourn while the world rejoices. You will grieve, but your grief will turn to joy" (John 16:20). If ever there was a message of hope for the lonely and the brokenhearted this Christmas, it's this. While the rest of the world seems to be throwing a party that we can't embrace or get behind because of the hurt of our life, Jesus promises it won't always be so.

In this context of giving and receiving love, joy is grown.

It's this intentionality of naming our expectations combined with the intentionality of abiding in God's love and loving those around me that might produce a sense of deep-seated pleasure—joy. I may not automatically feel it, but knowing the promise that it's on the way is a first step.

My Actual Approach

- Acknowledge my grief
- Host two Christmas parties
- Read the Christmas story daily

What I Will Be Reading

Isaiah 35:1–10

Luke 2:1–20

SUNDAY

We'd had this day marked on our calendar for a month. The littles, my mom, and I put on our Christmas velvet to go to *The Nutcracker* downtown at the Opera House. It was enough to make me jump out of bed . . . with joy.

This was the first time these two Kuykendall girls had been to the ballet, much less *The Nutcracker*. It was also the first time my mom had been to the show in years without Grandpa next to her. And so in some ways it felt bittersweet.

My mom and I shared a glass of wine in the Opera House lobby to toast the celebration. Gracelynn complained our second balcony seats were up too high. And we talked through expectations and being grateful to be there and how we weren't going to complain about what we could not change.

Bittersweet.

I've determined I'm not going to ignore the difficult in this week of joy. Yet I hung on to the sweet. How sweet to be able to take my girls to something indulgent, luxury filled, when mothers around the world would never get this chance. Sweet that my girls sat on the edge of their seats the first half (and laid across my lap the second, asking when it was going to be over and letting out heavy sighs as each new act came on). Sweet that afterwards we went to the crowded café next to the Opera House and ordered huge chocolate croissants with other performance goers, dancers in their street clothes, and orchestra members in their black dresses, and mingled and watched the bundled city goers go by.

The sweet outweighed the bitter for this afternoon. And I let that be enough. For today.

MONDAY

I woke up at 4:30, my brain whizzing with its to-do list items pressing in on me. I tried to will myself to go back to sleep. But no mental mind tricks could convince my body to obey. I was awake.

So I got up and started in on the dirty dishes in the sink. But there was no Cinderella-like birds' singing surrounding me, just tension and stress and *How will I possibly get it all done?* on the tip of my mind and my muscles.

Joy. Where is it in the days like this? When life feels as if it is suffocating me with responsibilities?

In the kitchen later that day, after many things were accomplished—executed if you will, but not much pleasure was had in the executing—I snapped at Derek because he smelled like smoke. He is a smoker. Not of the cigarette variety, but of the meat variety. In our backyard, with a black metal meat cooker-thing that is a mystery to me, he was out preparing food. You know, warm, tasty, nutritious food for us to eat for dinner, and I was staying inside our warm home complaining about it.

No more complaining about anything. It really doesn't help with the joy.

At the same time, one of the girls looked up from my phone, where she was checking the weather forecast and said, "It's not going to snow on Christmas."

Our silence did not mirror her apparent devastation. She wanted to make sure we understood the gravity of the news, "Christmas won't be the same."

Yep, right there in our kitchen my daughter and I managed, within thirty seconds, to complain about good food to eat and the fact that there won't be a fresh coat of snow on our Denver streets on Christmas morning. *Spoiled* might be the word that comes to mind right about now. And Derek was done.

"There's no complaining about Christmas!" he said to us.

Our blank stares must have convinced him we needed more.

"From this point forward, there's no complaining about Christmas."

"But I wasn't talking about Christmas," I answered. His look was all I needed.

No more complaining about anything. It really doesn't help with the joy.

TUESDAY

So is there a little bit about faking it until you make it when it comes to joy? Meaning you go through the motions of celebrating, even if you don't feel like it, because eventually your attitude will follow?

I've been stuffing some grief the last few months. I recognize the busy keeps me from feeling. It's a coping mechanism, perhaps not a healthy one, but it is one. One that doesn't necessarily feel like joy.

I'm reading from the second chapter of Luke this week. Trying my best to marinate in the Christmas story by reading it daily. There are two verses butted up right next to each other that each tell a complete story on their own.

> But Mary treasured up all these things and pondered them in her heart. The shepherds returned, glorifying and praising God for all the things they had heard and seen, which were just as they had been told. (Luke 2:19–20)

Here Mary has just given birth to God from her very human womb in a very (I'm assuming) stinky barn. She is trying to take it all in: that postpartum-exhaustion, hormone-filled, trying-to-get-the-baby-to-latch-on kind of moment, and she wants to remember it all. Oh, how I know that feeling. It may not all be perfect, but it's that touch of heaven I want to capture in my heart forever. I have so been there.

And then the shepherds were on their own kind of high, running through the streets, yelling, "Y'all are never going to believe this! God showed up in the craziest way!" What adrenaline they must have felt when they realized what they had just been a part of. And that the story was not over. Because this changed everything!

These two verses right next to each other, the new mother, perhaps the same age as my eldest daughter, quietly trying to make sense of it all, and the raucous shepherds clanging the bells and whooping and hollering. Both joy? Both taking pleasure in who God is and what he has done? Yes.

I don't think Mary was faking it until she felt it. I suspect she needed it to all sink in before she got up and danced. Besides, joy can be quiet and steady. And she'd just delivered a baby.

Joy can be quiet and steady.

Perhaps that's where I am in my grief. Grateful to have known a man who was strong and faithful, to have shared more than half of my life with him, yet still in a place of shock, of letting it all sink in. This life and death and gratitude and goodness. All joy? Yes, perhaps.

WEDNESDAY

The Christmas cards, those little love notes with HOPE inscribed across the front, have been my late-night project. The same evening I brought the cards home, I went on my phone, found a picture, and had it printed at the hour-photo at the pharmacy down the street. Look at me. Bam! Just knocking this task out. No perfectly designed cards. No professional photo shoot. No matching outfits. Just us sitting in front of our fireplace, in a slightly awkward position, but all of our eyes are open. The Christmas miracles just keep coming.

But now a few days later, as I taped photo after photo inside the cards, I started to hear my internal critical voice. *This image is a bit grainy. I should have lightened it. And cropped out our feet—Genevieve isn't wearing any shoes.* Suddenly all I could see with each photo I taped in were Genevieve's white socks. *Is this really the best image I want to put out in the world? To people who only see one picture of us a year? Who may even put this up on their fridge the next twelve months to think of our family?*

And then . . . No complaining about Christmas!

I mean, really? Sometimes I'm embarrassed by myself. Is this what I want our Christmas card to be about? A marketing tool for our gorgeous selves?! My very rebellion against this thinking was the reason I chose this card in the first place. HOPE. That baby in the manger right there in the middle of the O. A love note for our friends of HOPE and blessing for the Christmas season and the coming year. If I'm going to fixate on the photo, I probably shouldn't include one at all.

This relearning process didn't stop last week. Life is a work and a rework over and over. A little bit of missing the point creeps in, and the conscious mind game of going back to joy. Finding pleasure in the stuffing of the envelopes. That we have so many people we love who partner with us in work, ministry, and life. Pleasure in the girls sitting next to me who I have convinced to tape photos into the inside of the cards. Pleasure that we are warm and safe.

Back to the lyrics of that joy-centered Christmas carol: "Let every heart prepare him room." I picture my heart filled with all its gunk and imagine pushing the gunk aside in order to make space for Emmanuel, God with us. There might be a corner dedicated to him now, but my heart must prepare for proper room.

"He rules the world with truth and grace." I can't help but notice the present tense in this phrase. He rules the world today. This baby, who grew up to fulfill his mission on the cross so he could affirm, "It is finished."[2]

"And heaven and nature sing." Because he rules the world, all of his creation rejoices. That's it. It doesn't say heaven and nature sing when the Christmas card is beautiful and perfectly photoshopped, but because he rules the world. That's it then. Joy does really come back to Jesus.

Lord, I am grateful for the messy. For the white socks. For the awkward pose. For the uninspiring background. I thank you for the wrinkles. The extra pounds. For the uncombed hair. For the cards purchased at Walmart. For the grainy photo. For it ALL, Lord. For it all.

THURSDAY

A whiplash moment. I sat at the dining table with my laptop open reading my Facebook feed. Another description of the current geopolitical atrocities happening in a far-off place, of women and children currently being slaughtered on the other side of the world. As in today. Right now. Posts of the global community calling for a stop and prayers of mercy and grace being offered, friends speaking the frustration of our own limitations as average citizens to get anything done, and larger questions of how to live in an upside-down world.

And then Gracie said, "I love this song."

I looked up from my computer to see her running over to the speaker to turn up the volume. I stood up, because I too love this song. A little Justin Timberlake to get the morning started. By the time we got to the third line in the lyrics we were both in full dance mode. Because it's a song you just can't not dance to.

As we held hands while she stood on the kitchen stool, the joy on my girl's face was pure. So incredibly happy to be dancing in her pajamas with her mama on a cold morning before school. As I moved my arms and feet and gazed into her smile, the whiplash was continuing in my heart. Here our total spontaneous fun was juxtaposed with the stories I was reading seconds earlier about mothers and their babies fleeing gunfire.

One of the difficult mysteries of this life is how a generous, merciful God allows the disparity of this world. That I have been born into the circumstances I have. That there are entire nations in upheaval while my daughter and I rock out to JT and the makings of breakfast are spread across the kitchen counter. Is it okay to be joyful when others are not? I've heard that after losing someone many people feel guilty about being happy again. I also know I experience a lot of first-world guilt.

But that guilt can be pushed toward gratitude.

Lord, thank you for this healthy child with ears that hear music and legs to dance.

Thank you for a safe neighborhood and a political climate that is whacky yet stable.

Thank you that our basic needs are met every day. Every single one of them.

And from that gratitude comes action.

Lord use me today. My money, yours. My voice, yours as well. My influence in any way.

Prayer is something. And so is sending Derek off to do his work of providing homes for those coming out of the cold. One of my jobs is to support him as he does his work, his current assignment here on earth. But there are so many ways I'm called to influence my world, assignments of my own.

To offer my talents when needed.

To write a check.

To make a call.

To invite someone in, to conversation or my home, or both.

To make a meal.

To write a book.

And to dance in my kitchen with gratitude.

Because Lord, I take none of this for granted. Being grateful is part of what I can do in the midst of the despair. The action I can take that counters the evil in this world.

If love is action, joy stems from that place of action too. If I am to be setting the table for joy, meeting others' needs is certainly part of the process. And being grateful is a way of fighting back.

FRIDAY

I decided the little girls needed a new curtain rod f[c] room. It broke this summer, and today there was a sud[c] to have this detail fixed. You know, an hour before our gu[ ] for Derek's work party.

It was a double party day. Yes, two parties in our house in a single calendar day. Because if we're going to do all of the cleaning, decluttering, and organizing required to have one group over, why not make that two?

So the Prov staff came for lunch. They brought the food and paper plates. I just needed to offer a clean, warm house with welcoming places to talk and eat.

I read a quote this morning by author Karen Ehman: "Entertaining puts the emphasis on you and your home and seeks to impress others. In contrast, hospitality puts the emphasis on your guest and seeks to help them to feel refreshed, not impressed, when they leave your home."[3] If there ever was a group of people I wanted to put the emphasis on, to help feel more loved when they left than when they arrived, it was this group. They are easy to please, for sure. They live with people coming out of shelters, they are pretty accepting of mess. And they give their lives to make family for others. They deserved my best version of rolling out the red carpet to celebrate Christmas.

Being grateful is part of what I can do in the midst of the despair.

I make it sound so easy-breezy, don't I? Like I'm so comfortable with a group of twenty coming and seeing every nook and cranny of our house. Should I mention that in the last week Derek finished the trim around the kitchen ceiling vent (installed this past summer), he painted the hallway and two walls in the house that were covered in grimy fingerprints and drawings from our resident preschool artists,

I had the carpets cleaned and the house cleaned, and we switched out sofas from the basement to the upstairs?

For two weeks we've been preparing for this day. It was like our Super Bowl of this Christmas season's entertaining. And it involved much more fanfare than I would like to admit. Because I would like to be a bit more easy-breezy about it all. So I spent my teensy party budget where I knew it would keep me the most sane: not on fancy holiday decorations or party favors, but on three angels who came for 90 minutes the morning of the parties to clean my toilets and vacuum lines into my carpets.

Our dinner gathering that night was a few families with enough people among us to make it a party. Jen, Kristi, and Crystal's families. Our eldest children were born around the same time. We've grown up into parenting together and have multiplied many times over with kids who are in the middle of making high school decisions and in a few years will be leaving for college.

We have only a few Christmas seasons left with this group when everyone is still at home. With kids wanting to decorate cookies and hang out in the basement, and boys not sure how to talk to girls who aren't their sisters. We had the white elephant gift exchange where the crowd roared when *that* kid got the Ken doll or *that* dad got the earwax cleaning kit and the "Steal it! Steal it!" chants made sure the neighbors were still awake (because we are good parents and have agreed that stealing is part of our collective value system).

As we finished dinner, with the adults alone at the table, a wrapped box was placed on my plate: wind chimes to hang on my back patio in remembrance of Grandpa. I'm a crier by nature, so my tears were expected on this gift opening. But as I said, I've been perfecting my emotional stuffing skills. So the tears this time were shed by those around me on my behalf as I unwrapped the chimes. "You can think of him every time you hear them," Crystal said.

Sitting in the middle of that hubbub I knew the two weeks of cleaning had been worth it. If I'm going to have my carpets shampooed, I might as well throw a party so everyone else can enjoy them before they will inevitably get dirty again. But mostly as everyone ran through the falling snow to their cars and I began to load the dishwasher, I was grateful beyond belief to do life next to people who love God and love others. Some of my guests for the day know me as well as anyone, and others I'd met for the first time. Today was the literal setting of the table in our home, ready for joy to unfold.

Preparing for joy is part tactical execution, part heart work.

Perhaps preparing for joy is part tactical execution, part heart work. Either way, a house full of people makes for a great way to celebrate.

Saturday

We woke up to continued snow falling and subzero temperatures. I made the coffee, turned on the fire, and thanked God for a slow morning. The wind chimes blew in the snow outside. A reminder of Grandpa and friendship.

How does this joy/grief paradox work? Can they coexist? John 16, with Jesus now grown, uses an illustration I can relate to: "A woman giving birth to a child has pain because her time has come; but when her baby is born she forgets the anguish because of her joy that a child is born into the world."[4] Well that feels familiar four times over. If ever there was a picture of pain ending in joy that stems from my actual life, it's this one.

Jesus continues, "So with you: Now is your time of grief, but I will see you again and you will rejoice, and no one will take away your joy."[5] This is not a promise of immediate relief, but of a big-picture resolution where things will get better, will be easier. I may not be able to see past today's circumstances, but the knowledge of Jesus's promise is what I can hold on to. It does ultimately come back to him, doesn't it? This Christmas story pushes toward a larger

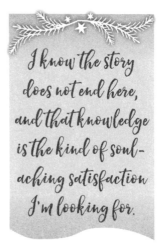

I know the story does not end here, and that knowledge is the kind of soul-aching satisfaction I'm looking for.

story: one of a grown-up baby who makes our joy full, how everything changed at his birth, at the cross, and will change again at his return.

This time of year we hang out in the manger scene with the shepherds and the wise men. And like those shepherds, we know the story isn't over; it's still unfolding. I can sit with my own grief in these days. I know the story does not end here, and that knowledge is the kind of soul-aching satisfaction I'm looking for. Joy is more than the fleeting happy that I'm constantly trying to re-create; it is the satisfying knowledge of the unchanging, life-altering story of Christmas.

What I Learned

I'm thinking about the word *enjoy*. *En* in Spanish means "in." To "enjoy" is to be in joy. This has been a week of not avoiding my actual life, the grief and stress, but acknowledging my circumstances and actively choosing to invite joy in. This is not so much a feeling as it is a posture. One of celebrating the good that is in my actual circumstances and remembering this story is one of redemption.

It has been a week of finding pleasure in the Christmas I have this year. The one planted firmly in the middle of my regular chaos. And if I ever needed to have use of something, it's the Christmas story. Long ago this turn of events changed history. But it's not just an old story. It is for my heart and benefit today. Mary and Joseph, weary parents submitting to circumstances they didn't expect and that were out of their control, was for my benefit. And this tiny baby who would grow to be a man who would speak words that would change history and live beyond the cross? For my benefit as well.

To experience joy this week was to stand in agreement that yes, I need this season as a recalibration for my year. That coffee and quiet and snow are things to be grateful for. A sleeping family, food in the fridge, God's love—all things I don't want to take for granted. And I also thank him for the tears and pain. For the memories of the bittersweet variety. It's not so much that joy is a choice as it is a reflection of the active posture to take pleasure in God and his world and to love those around me. Joy is deeper than the fleeting magic the season has to offer. Fortunately, Christmas has more to do with the lasting than the temporary.

Practices I'll Continue

- No complaining about Christmas
- Select Christmas cards that act as love notes to their recipients
- Host at least two Christmas gatherings in our home
- When possible, outsource practical help so I can enjoy the activities

QUESTIONS FOR REFLECTION

1. What are the pains or hurts you carry this Christmas season?
2. Describe a "whiplash moment" when the world felt difficult and beautiful at once. How do you make sense of the contrast?
3. How do you think the Christmas story points to a larger story of joy for the world? For your life?

Words for My Actual Christmas

Very truly I tell you, you will weep and mourn while the world rejoices. You will grieve, but your grief will turn to joy. (John 16:20)

ADVENT WEEK 4

Peace

While you are proclaiming peace with your lips,
be careful to have it even more fully in your heart.

—Francis of Assisi

The Need

It's crunch time around here. The details that are still undone must be attended to. Time is slipping away, and the to-do list remains long. Then I remember details that aren't even on the list. *Stockings! Teacher gifts! And those last Christmas cards whose addresses I still need to track down.* This is when the stress not only creeps in, it's full blown. It's the point in the season when I give in and decide I'm in survival mode. *I'm going to need to blow the budget, to not sleep, to eat cookies for dinner, because I have to power through. This is the week I will be stressed. Because who are we kidding anyway? It's Christmas and we all know Christmas is stressful!*

But the whole point of this experiment is to end this kind of thinking. To right-size my expectations and to live in the circumstances in front of me, fully embracing the themes of the season. And this week that theme is peace.

Peace is a sense of calm, harmony, and a freedom from war. All something I need more of around here. When I'm up until midnight on Christmas Eve frantically wrapping gifts or making the egg casserole, I must remember a sense of calm, harmony, and freedom from war is my aim. I can't resign myself to be stressed and accept it as inevitable and also live in peace. The two paths are mutually exclusive. And since I follow the Prince of Peace,[1] I must have access to some of that peace, right?

The Experiment

I know this will be a week of letting go. Of releasing expectations, plans, and ideas of how I think things *should* happen. Of going with the flow, being flexible. Because there will always be more to do: more details to attend to, more bows to tie, more cleaning and cooking and decorating that could be done. And none of those things bring peace if done with frantic zeal. In fact, they won't bring peace at all. I don't need an experiment to tell me that. Those final touches are the icing on the Christmas cake; Christmas will happen, regardless.

However, peace won't happen on its own. I must be active in the prioritizing and the letting go. If I don't add some intentionality here, the monster that is the Christmas to-do list will take over and I will buckle under its pressure. Hardly a peaceful way to go down.

My Actual Approach

- Modify or eliminate activities that will cause me avoidable stress
- Take care of my physical needs: sleep, exercise, healthy eating
- Get all wrapping and shopping done by the 22nd

What I Will Be Reading

Isaiah 9:1–7

Mark 12:24–37

SUNDAY

Today ended with one of my favorite Christmas traditions: the pageant party. But in order to make it to the party I had lots of running from one thing to the next.

There was working out (the first time in a long while I've done anything other than walk on the treadmill), getting everyone ready and out the door to church (with breakfast and snow boots and digging out the truck from the snowstorm the day before), teaching Sunday school (of course cramming the lesson plan as children were arriving in the classroom), coming home, making lunch, doing a few dishes, heading to a Broncos game viewing party at Derek's parents' (aka Oma and Opa's) house, going to Target to get some gifts for the party that night, wrapping gifts, preparing tamales (by preparing I mean warming in the microwave and cutting in half), getting everyone changed into Christmas dresses, and—phew—making it to the annual pageant party.

This tradition is as close to *A Charlie Brown Christmas* as my real life gets. A Christmas party that includes a pageant with costumes and half-memorized lines and the audience sings Christmas carols between scenes. Where the curtain is a sheet, the stage a dining room, and the set a lit star hanging from the ceiling by a cord. The actors are children, and the audience has a high camera–per capita count and is sitting on top of each other in the living room with the sofas and chairs all turned toward the dining room opening. And for a moment I feel like I can breathe as we all focus in on the famous story.

Just like the original story, it is cast with a real baby. This year the actress cried the whole time she was on "stage," with a young Mary who wasn't sure what to do (I'm assuming a lot like the real

⭐ *See: Stewarding the Story, page 126.*

Mary in those ways). The kids act as shepherds and even sheep, and absorb the idea of these characters from so long ago as real people who said real words.•

We haven't missed the annual pageant since Gabi was baby Jesus fourteen years ago. That first year I was hesitant when my mother-in-law, Carol, asked me to bring my precious newborn to this party and pass her over to a coughing tweenager. But all I needed were a few photos of my daughter in swaddling clothes and this mama was hooked. And after the cast is changed back into their Christmas finest, Santa comes bearing gifts. The best kind of cast party, really.

This is the Christmas season. To pause from the hustle and remember.

I am never sad we've made this event a priority amid the rush of the season. This party Derek attended and acted in as a child. In the midst of the hustle, it's a collective pause, peace for my spirit in the holiday storm. A community remembrance of this tale that our hearts need every year. This is the Christmas season. To pause from the hustle and remember.

MONDAY

Of course the tasks still need to get done. I need ribbon for ornaments, last-minute presents I'm sending in the mail, and supplies to make teacher gifts for the last day of school. The hustle from the day before hasn't disappeared. Neither has the story from the night before.

"Away in a Manger," "We Three Kings," and "Silent Night" still linger in my head and heart. Yes, I need to run around and check some to-dos off my list today, but they can be done within the framework of a grateful and full heart.

It turns out my body is in slight shock from yesterday's workout, confirming I'm not the best at taking care of my physical needs. Further confirmed by the "What's for dinner?" questions aimed my way as Gabi and I are walking out the door at 6:30 p.m. for some Christmas shopping. I have no answer. I forgot about dinner. That it would be required at all. Things have reached a desperation point.

It's 8:00 p.m., and I'm serving up mini quiches pulled from the freezer and warmed in the oven. I'm chopping up red bell peppers I determined weren't spoiled yet. I'm sautéing a bag of spinach with garlic. There are vegetables, I guess that's good. Kids might be falling asleep as they eat them, but there are vegetables! I need to do a better job of the basics here. Rest. Exercise. Food. Or we may not make it until Christmas morning.

Now off to bed, children. Two more days of school and then you are home with me for two and a half weeks. This mama needs some sleep if there's going to be any kind of peace around here.

Tuesday

Here we go with normal life butting up against Christmas life. As I wake up, I begin laundry and dishes and picking up toys. Another party at our house tonight—a birthday party! Because yes, December birthdays still happen. My niece Karis turns 12 today, and we are having a surprise dinner celebration here.

My last day to wrap gifts and shop without children's eyes watching. My last day to attend to the Christmas orchestrating alone. And we interrupt this Christmas season to have a birthday party to celebrate a precious life. There is some overlap between the season and this party. This is all about celebrating life.

Though we want to keep this party very "birthday," no comingling with the Christmas holiday, my posture of celebrating life is the same. Right here with birthday candles and cake and ice cream and non-Christmas wrapping paper we are surrounded by a tree and stockings and gingerbread houses from a week and a half ago that are drying out and beginning to lose their gumdrops. Icing is flaking off the roofs just as the needles are beginning to drop from the drying tree.

Right in the middle of this Christmas mess we have a party with screaming kids and siblings that argue. Oma and Opa who hide behind the couch to yell surprise and cousins who have a hard time staying quiet before the big reveal. Just as Jesus was born right in the middle of the cow manure and goats that wouldn't stop bleating and hay that likely aggravated Mary's allergies. No midwife. No epidural. No warming blankets. I've been in a delivery room, I know the mess that is made. There was nothing neat and tidy. Fully human and fully divine, he entered the world like the rest of us.

Happy birthday, Karis. Happy birthday, Jesus. Life and celebration right in the middle of our actual messy lives. I look over at the drying, dying tree. It seems we are all hanging on, hoping to make it to the 25th around here. There is something built into us that yearns for the Prince of Peace and it feels especially potent today.

WEDNESDAY

Who knew the internet would offer me insights on peace today? Especially since the headlines scream of the world's upside-down nature. Anything but peaceful.

As I scrolled through my Facebook feed this morning, looking at pictures of screaming toddlers on Santa's lap and snowsuit-bundled children making forts, I read this from pastor and author Eugene Cho:

> During the Advent season, we often talk about Peace . . . and rightfully so. As Christians, we should care deeply about peace but all too often, our simple answer to the need for peace is "It's a sin issue" and thus, we need a transformation of the heart. Yes, I agree: It's indeed a sin issue and absolutely, Jesus is our great Reconciler and we must preach the good news that "Jesus saves!" but if we reduce sin merely to a personal issue, we neglect the reality of what happens when sin becomes communal and as such, creates systems, institutions, and

culture. Both are essential if we're about the whole Gospel and the Kingdom of God.

In other words, there's a difference between peace-making and peace-keeping. It's a subtle but dangerous mentality if our definition of peace-making is really peace-keeping—as in, "Peace. Peace. Let's keep peace. Let's not rock the boat. It's working well for me."[2]

I paused the scrolling. I've had a pretty self-focused view of peace the last few days. How do I make my life more peaceful, easier really, in the midst of the Christmas chaos? Am I completely missing the point? Does my idea of peace mean maintaining the status quo? Not rocking the boat? Who gains as a result? Me and my own comfort? Who is hurt by my peacekeeping?

Jesus was not much of a peacekeeper. He was more of the peacemaker variety, which often looked a lot like causing waves (or calming seas, I guess). His very arrival in the manger was not about maintaining the status quo, it was all about turning it upside-down. Not only did he enter the world in full birth messiness, he entered a world that was in full political chaos. His parents were refugees, moving to be counted in the census, and then later escaping to keep him from being executed.

> His very arrival in the manger was not about maintaining the status quo, it was all about turning it upside-down.

I thought of the day's headlines of women and children being killed. "History repeats itself" is not just a quippy phrase. I again considered the refugees, the governments turning on their own people, and wondered, how do I become a peacemaker here?

Lord Jesus, thank you for coming to turn the systems upside-down. To teach us that the last shall become first. Show me how to be the hands and feet of peacemaking in your world. In my home. On my block. In my church. In your church. In my circles of influence. May I stand in the uncomfortable, the awkward, the controversial in order to speak what is right. Lord help me to move away from self-preservation and toward Holy Spirit magnification with my words, actions, posture, and thoughts. –Amen

If all was joy, we likely wouldn't recognize it.

Then tonight, in between telling the sleepover girls to quiet down again (yes, a fifth-grade slumber party to celebrate the beginning of Christmas break—not really helpful in the getting-good-sleep department), I watched a short film by animator Corrie Francis Parks. Grains of sand moved and danced across the screen, making formations that quickly disappeared before new ones were quickly formed. She explained why she uses sand as her medium.

> When the camera is pulled back, it is the light which illuminates the chiaroscuro of a delicate sand drawing and defines the stark silhouette of sculpted piles of sands. Light transforms an ordinary material into something worthy of contemplation. Without the light, the sand is inert, dull and invisible. Without the sand, the light is blinding, formless, colorless. And here we find the truer paradox: the sand is the only way we can effectively see, understand and enjoy the light.[3]

The sand is the only way we can see the light! But of course. Our pain, grief, disappointment juxtaposes with the joy and peace so we can actually see it and believe it exists. If all was joy, we likely wouldn't recognize it. In many ways the hard of this actual Christmas allows me to see, or experience, the peace as well.

THURSDAY

We had a single mission today: making cookies. Five recipes, four girls to help, and one grandma to add in the merriment made for an all-hands-working, relaxed-pace kind of day. As I cleaned up, I congratulated myself on planning only a single activity for one of these last days before Christmas. No jam-packed schedule. One thing. It allowed us to take our time. To focus. To be in this moment without rushing to the next. I was more relaxed than cookie makings past. I set the expectation that everyone participate (since they requested to have this baking session in the first place). Yes, perhaps peace is simply building time into the schedule. And then exercising to make up for all of that cookie dough.

See: The Power of No Thank You, page 111.

Later as I waited to pull out of the grocery store parking lot, the car behind me honked. I knew it was at me for taking too long as I waited to make a left-hand turn.

Okay, so maybe I'm a little bit of a tortoise-like driver, maybe I get honked at semi-frequently. But this stood out to me because, well . . . it's Christmas! Can we get a little bit of brotherly/sisterly love here? Some peace?

And as I heard the driver rev his engine, I could feel the tension in his life. It's unavoidable—this stress of our walking around on earth. I understand it. Only minutes earlier, I wanted to sit down in the middle of the grocery store and let it all out. First there were the bags of Cuties, mini-oranges, on display when I first walked in. Grandpa, born during the Depression, always had a single orange in his stocking as a child. A splurge by the day's standards. Something we referenced and would sneak into his more recent stockings.

Minutes later I held back tears as I stood in the seasonal candy aisle trying to decide if I should buy my mom a box of chocolates on behalf of her husband gone only a few months. I'd done his Christmas shopping for him the last few years—I knew what regulars were on the list—and I stood there and wondered if it would make her feel better or worse if I bought her a box and wrote his name on the tag. I felt the tears forming and turned my cart so I could walk away and maybe leave the feelings behind with the floor-to-ceiling boxes of Almond Roca.

So I get it, car behind me! We all are having a heck of a moment. You have no idea what I'm leaving behind in that grocery store . . . and I guess I don't know what you are either.

Stopping and recognizing I didn't know what was truly behind the impatience of the anonymous honker helped me feel a bit more sympathetic as I shook my head rather than my fist. Some churches pass the peace as they shake hands on a Sunday morning with a greeting of "Peace be with you." Let this be my passing of the peace, extending grace wherever and to whomever possible. Because we're all a little on edge these days.

FRIDAY

Wrapping. Gift counting. Organizing.

"Where is that Buffs hat for Genevieve?" I half whispered to Derek.

"I don't think it came." He matched my whisper.

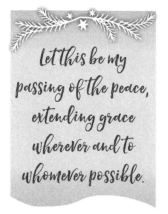

Let this be my passing of the peace, extending grace wherever and to whomever possible.

"Wait, you told me it did." I made hand motions for the buffalo horns on the furry buffalo hat we'd ordered to remind him.

"*That* one came. The other one, the stocking cap, I don't think it did."

"Oh, I think it did. You hid it."

"Where?"

"I don't know. *You* hid it."

Yes, today is a day of looking through our house for gifts that arrived the last few weeks via Amazon. We quickly hid them away from peeking eyes and climbing children and in the process can't remember where we've put them.

Every year. It's our own little tradition.

Exhibit A of first-world problems in our first-world Christmas: we have so many gifts we don't remember what we've purchased. And our house is so big we can't find them all.

Sheesh. No stress allowed over our issues today. None. #nocomplainingaboutChristmas

I'm not sure how long I cried on the kitchen floor, but it was long enough that the papers in my hand were soaked and the ink was bleeding.

It started with an argument. Derek mentioned getting some things for the girls' stockings. My mom had just taken the girls away to a movie, and I'd spent those hours counting and recounting gifts, wrapping, making sure to use special Santa paper for the Santa gifts, making last-minute notes on my final Walmart run for batteries or one more item for a particular girl's stocking.

And then he came home and was so casual about picking up a few things for stockings, and the anger came blazing out of my mouth like dragon fire. I had a system. I'd been planning this for weeks. I was making notes, for crying out loud. And he went and "bought a few things"?!

His reaction to my reaction clued me in that maybe I was over-reacting. "What happened to loving your actual Christmas?" he asked. "This seems to be stress you've created for yourself."

I didn't like his tone. And those obviously true statements were not helpful. He left the room and I went searching for the cookbook that had the egg casserole I always made for Christmas morning. Because that egg casserole wasn't going to make itself and this number one Christmas orchestrator needed to keep the party moving in the right direction.

The tears started and at first felt like a normal kind of fight cry. But they kept coming. And the air wasn't passing in and out of my body naturally. My focus moved from tears to the basics of breathing. It was becoming clear this wasn't a regular fight cry, there was something else going on. And suddenly clarity: this had to do with control.

I can control these Christmas details. The gifts. The stockings. The egg casserole. I can't control the grief, my mom's grief, the obvious empty places where we are used to seeing Grandpa.

The latching on to the stocking list wasn't about the stockings at all. It was about controlling a part of Christmas that I thought I could. And anyone who got between me and my gift count (read: Derek) was going to feel it.

Suddenly, I didn't want to make the egg casserole. That recipe I always made on Christmas and Easter and rarely anytime else. I had an abrupt and unexpected aversion to it. It was a symbol of years past. And things were now different. How could I pretend like everything was okay, making that same casserole like I always did, as if nothing had happened?

"So don't make it," Derek said as he was rubbing my back a few minutes later. I'd picked myself up off of the kitchen floor, gone into our room, apologized for the dragon fire, and explained the inner fire that was its source.

He was right: don't make it. If the egg casserole is going to be a cause of grief this year, there is no reason to hang on to it. My load felt a smidge lighter. There is much that is out of my control right now, but I can control this. Wipe the tears, deep breaths. *Prince of Peace, come near.*

SATURDAY

We went to see Santa at Union Station downtown this morning. It felt festive and like the right thing to do. We arrived when the big guy did, but the line to visit and sit on his lap was already wrapped around the inside of the historic train station. We all agreed we could mail Santa his letters and they would still get there by the evening. So we had coffee and scones and sat near the main attraction and watched babies scream as they were handed over to the man in red.

I went home and made the egg casserole. The permission to not do it was all I needed to take its power away. Besides, Genevieve, who rarely makes a special request, asked for our Christmas morning breakfast tradition. That gave it new purpose; I was making it for her.

"On earth peace to those on whom his favor rests."

The Christmas Eve service at church was full. We were late and sat in the back where the ushers were adding folding chairs to make more rows for the latecomers. And the familiar words from the reading pierced my heart.

> But the angel said to them, "Do not be afraid. I bring you good news that will cause great joy for all the people. Today in the town of David a Savior has been born to you; he is the Messiah, the Lord. This will be a sign to you: You will find a baby wrapped in cloths and lying in a manger."
>
> Suddenly a great company of the heavenly host appeared with the angel, praising God and saying,
>
> "Glory to God in the highest heaven,
>   and on earth peace to those on whom his favor rests."
>   (Luke 2:10–14)

The passing of the light from candle to candle moved from the front of the room toward the latecomer section. I could see sweet faces illuminated by the candles they held. Soft and warm light dancing on each God-inspired, God-created face.

Wipe tears, deep breaths. *Prince of Peace, come near.*

What I Learned

Though the stress of this last week leading up to the main event of Christmas Day was somewhat unavoidable, I was more at peace than I remember in years past. I could feel the benefits of the experiment. I'd paced myself with the practical. Although all my shopping wasn't complete by the 22nd (there was a final run to Walmart on the 24th), I was much further along than I would have been had I not set that goal at the beginning of the week. Pacing out our activities, one main event per day, also helped. The peace that came from an intentional schedule was evident.

Scheduling, taking care of my (and my family's) physical needs, and eliminating responsibilities that add to my stress are all tactical approaches I can take to add peace to our family. Lifting my head above my immediate circumstances reminds me that the world is not inherently a peaceful place. Not every woman is approaching Christmas Day with the same circumstances I am. This perspective reminds me to be grateful for the literal peace in my community and home and to be mindful of those around me, near and far, who are searching for internal and external peace. My gratitude increases when I'm in this place, and the question that echoes around me is, how can I work to be more of a peacemaker in my immediate circle and the larger world?

See: Saving Time for What's Most Important, page 105.

I come to the 25th with a renewed understanding of peace and an intensified thirst for the Prince of Peace to reign right here in my actual life. But nothing settles this frenzied Christmas heart like remembering the story. The setting, the characters, the plot and its twists. When I do, my own Christmas story, the one I'm living out in real time, has a different purpose. The discipline of being in the story—reading it, hearing it told through the traditional carols, watching it played out by actors—pushes through to my heart through various channels. The written word, music, sight and sound, color and texture all come together to make this tale more alive and real. It's when I'm placed in the middle of this scene that the world makes a little more sense. My soul recalibrates, and I'm able to face the current chaos that is my life, my heart, and my world.

Practices I'll Continue

- Have holiday meals planned, and when possible prepped, ahead of time
- Get consistent sleep
- Set a gift shopping deadline (and designated hiding spots)
- Attend the Christmas Eve service at church

QUESTIONS FOR REFLECTION

1. What adds to your stress this last week before Christmas? Is there a way you can change or eliminate this source of stress?
2. Do you see yourself as a peacekeeper or a peacemaker? Which would you like to be? Why?
3. How can you find peace in the middle of the last-minute chaos?

Words for My Actual Christmas

> For to us a child is born,
>   to us a son is given,
>   and the government will be on his shoulders.
> And he will be called
>   Wonderful Counselor, Mighty God,
>   Everlasting Father, Prince of Peace. (Isaiah 9:6)

Christmastide

I will honor Christmas in my heart, and try to keep it all the year.

—Charles Dickens

The Need

This is how my Christmas typically plays out. Go, go, go, getting everything ready for the 25th. Collapse in a coma-like state on the 26th (perhaps thanking God that it is all over until next year's circus begins). I tend to make the 25th the pinnacle, everything builds up to that single day, when in reality I usually have more downtime between Christmas and New Year's to actually enjoy my people, my decorations, the Christmas message. It is time to unwind, to be quiet, and to absorb the Christmas story.

Here's the crazy thing: the church calendar has this extended Christmas season built into it. We call this stretch of days Christmastide, or the twelve days of Christmas. This period begins on Christmas morning and goes for twelve days, ending on January 6th with Epiphany and the arrival of the magi to the Baby Jesus. Not coming from a highly liturgical background, I just don't recognize these days as such. I tend to see them as that time for ski vacations or Christmas clearance, or just more long days when kids are home from school and I need to figure out how to entertain them and keep my yelling to a minimum.

But what if? What if I used these twelve days for Christmastide's intended purpose? To celebrate God's birth as a baby over an extended period of time? What if I reclaimed these twelve days as an exit from the current calendar year and entrance to the next, holding the spirit of Christmas at the forefront of my priorities? What if I gave baby Jesus the kind of attention his birth deserves instead of moving directly on to the next holiday? (Yes, when I was in Walmart on the 24th the employees were putting out Valentine's Day candy. Because Christmas Eve must mean it's time to move on, right?) What if I let my heart dwell a bit on this miracle I am remembering in the first place?

The Experiment

My hope is to use this stretch of days to re-center my heart. To stop and pay attention to what the Christmas story means for my life today and consider what might need to be different on a practical end in the coming year. A spiritual renewal time of quiet in my schedule that can prepare me a bit for the next twelve months.

There is already a natural carving out here with school on vacation and work life halted a bit. But I don't want to let these days disappear like they have in years past. I want to add some intentionality, to actively participate in this Christmastide—be a relisher, rather than a passive bystander. I declare that Christmas is this entire season, and since I'm in charge of my family's schedule, I have some control over how we spend it.

We will have downtime. We won't rush. We will keep the Christmas decorations up. We will feast, since many liturgical traditions refer to this time as a "feast" anyway. A celebration. So we will eat and revel. And we will let the themes we just left behind of hope, love, joy, and peace be our mantra for this time.

My Actual Approach

- Schedule unscheduled days
- Spend time cooking and eating together as a family and with friends
- Pack up Christmas—literally and figuratively—in a way that will make me happy when I unpack it next year

What I Will Be Reading

Matthew 2

Luke 2:22–52

DAY 1: CHRISTMAS DAY

We spent the morning with my mom and the evening at Oma and Opa's. A day as expected of gifts, more gifts, food, more food, family, more family, and a little football watching.

In our typical rhythm, Christmas Eve focused on the baby Jesus and Christmas Day on the gifts God has given us: our family and provision above our basic needs. Quite an understatement, as evidenced by the number of gifts and the tug on our waistlines. I'd say we sorely failed in sticking to that budget number Derek threw out a few weeks ago, but we were still within our comfort level. Well, we'll try again next year.

Because I'd prepared by actively pacing myself the last few weeks, today had a rested sense. A go-to-bed at a decent hour the night before (only a few late-night gifts to wrap) and wake up with the sun, not the pitch dark of night. (Though Derek did catch our girls Facetiming their cousins at 4:30 in the morning. Bless these children all anxiously awaiting their parents' minimum wake-up times while fully taking advantage of technology to communicate with one another.)

We had oranges as part of our menu in honor of Grandpa's Christmas orange and talked about him and missed him terribly. And we thanked God for the fullness of life right here and now and for a man with a life well lived. It was a hard day. A good day. An actual Christmas Day right smack-dab in the middle of our actual lives.

DAY 2: BOXING DAY

We woke up at Derek's parents' house, coffee in hand, Christmas jammies on, and the grown-ups' discussion turned to "Boxing Day." The day after Christmas, the 26th, known to our Canadian, Australian, and British friends (in other words, all our proper friends) as "Boxing Day." Although this is a shopping day in modern times, the name originated from the tradition of giving boxes to "the help" the day after Christmas. Boxes included a gift or tip or leftover Christmas treats for servants to take home to their own families to celebrate the holiday.[1]

This is certainly a day that feels relevant to the characters of *Downton Abbey*, and today's shopping twist keeps the "boxing" title appropriate, but it's all a new holiday to me. It seems to stem from a spirit of generosity, where people gather and give. I like that.

Though I won't head to the pub before or after the foxhunting excursion (both traditions as well), and I don't have any help to whom I need to send boxes of goodies, I will send a few messages to friends far away about how much I love and appreciate them. The ones I haven't run into in the last few weeks of festivities.

My little "boxes" will be inboxes of the email and voicemail variety—an American girl's take on Boxing Day.

DAYS 3–6: DECEMBER 27–30TH

A series of days spent lying around. Tearing down boxes, eating cookies, making blanket forts, and being with cousins. It was binge-watching *Friday Night Lights* and sleeping as long as the dog would allow. It was sneaking in time with friends who were in town visiting family, but mostly it was the option of staying in our pajamas for as long as we fancied.

Although this stretch looked much like years' past, I was intentional about the downtime. I made sure we were relaxing and relishing as much as we could with as little schedule as possible.

The girls had cousins over and we went to their houses. Neighbors came over and we went to play there too. A total freedom of agenda that is rare in our fast-paced, overly programmed lives. And we relished the lack of obligations. It seems a bit nonsensical to schedule in days that are unscheduled. But just like we all need daily downtime, we also need down days every season. These were our down days. My kids are bored? That's okay, it's good for them. They're getting sick of each other? Also okay. It will help build enthusiasm for us to start back to our regular crazy in a week.

My little "boxes" will be inboxes of the email and voicemail variety— an American girl's take on Boxing Day.

I tried to say yes as often as I could. Yes to friends. Yes to dessert. Yes to another episode. Because why not? This is a party, a birthday party for our King of Kings, and we should be acting as such. It makes me think of weddings or funerals in other countries that last ten days. Do we not have something to celebrate here? The Messiah. Emmanuel, God with us. In our world of overprogramming, perhaps a true celebration is to have a few days of vacation like this, where we indulge a bit in our favorite people, foods, activities. In the slowest pace possible— because who needs more stress?

It turns out the twelve nights of Christmas were originally intended to be an extended time of prayer and rest from unnecessary labor.[2] Twelve days to celebrate the Savior every year? I feel like that's the least we can do.

This is feasting.

Day 7: December 31st

Since the beginning of time (well, in my personal history, at least) New Year's Eve has been a letdown kind of holiday. Though I've had my years of fun and parties, it almost always seems to have a tinge of disappointment that the night didn't live up to expectations. Am I the only one?

Becoming a mom took away any preconceived ideas that the night would be an unforgettable one. A sitter, crowds, and overpriced drinks when it's freezing outside? Besides, staying up until midnight takes more and more work as the years go on.

I sit once again in the postures of the season: hope, love, joy, and peace.

For many New Year's Eve is one of those annual markers that reminds us of our circumstances, that ends a year where things are not as they should be. Life is not turning out the way we'd planned or expected. So as this actual year ends and time keeps rolling forward, I sit once again in the postures of the season: hope, love, joy, and peace. I set the table for these attributes in the coming year with an expectant heart.

Hope that I will encounter more of him in the next twelve months.

Love for my "neighbors," those under my roof and on the other side of the world.

Joy in the pleasure of what God has gifted me.

Peace that his authority is still final in this upside-down world.

Advent is the period of expectation and waiting. Christmastide is the season of celebrating his arrival. I celebrate here in the middle of my actual life with my actual circumstances.

Day 8: January 1st

Though my focus in this experiment is relishing the actual, I have to admit I'm a sucker for new beginnings. Fresh starts. I call it my inner social worker. Derek and I have renovated three homes, because . . . the potential! How can you not love a makeover? A redemption story of any type?

This obsession with the fresh start has to do with my faith. God is the expert in taking the old and making it new. The damaged becomes restored into something more beautiful than the original because of his magnificent touch.

Stepping into a new year, I can't help but think what new might unfold. Some is hard to fathom in a good way. My mom alone, trying to make her way as a single woman. Gabi going into high school, and Derek and I having to experience a new level of letting go. Not only that, we'll have one transitioning into middle school and my baby will start kindergarten. All major life moments that stir up more fear and doubt than genuine excitement.

But I know I don't have to wait for his change in me, his fine-tuning. He is making me new. Every year. Every month. Every day. He has moved into the neighborhood of my heart, and that I can count on, because I see glimmers of change.

Day 9: January 2nd

I couldn't wait another day.

I had to clean up Christmas.

Some I know use this Christmastide as the time to relish in the decorations and the music. And were the decorations not begging me to end their misery, I might have been able to make it a bit longer. But the tree was beyond dead, branches bent downward and the needles littering the floor. The poinsettias were wilting, drooping over, tired and ready for their retirement, dropping their crimson petals on the mantel. And the weather app was telling us the cold was returning. If I was going to take down the outdoor lights in the next week, today needed to be the day.

So I did my best to pack things up in a way that would make me happy to open the boxes the coming November. And you know what? I had no urges to stuff it all in. To wad up the lights and close the lids vowing to do Christmas differently next year. In fact, I was not over Christmas, it was almost the opposite; I was a bit sad that the season was coming to a close.

I pictured myself taking off the box lids nearly a year from now, uncoiling the neatly wound strings of lights, and wondered what life changes will have come. How will I be hungry for the story again? Will I be that haggard woman bracing myself for the coming crazy, or will I be spiritually refreshed? I don't know what state I'll be in, but I'm giving my next-year self a little gift by having (somewhat) organized containers of lights, ornaments, and Christmas plates.

Once I got going with this self–gift giving, I didn't want to stop. So I gave myself an early Christmas present. And it's a whopper. One that's years overdue: a Christmas card mailing address list. Two hours at the computer, and I put together a spreadsheet of addresses for next year's cards. It's not exhaustive, it's not in perfect order, but it's a start. How many texts did I send in the last month, emails that read, "I know I ask for this every year, but could I get your address again?" No more of that. Time to adult around here with records kept. From Christmases forward I will now refer to this as "the golden spreadsheet."

DAY 10: JANUARY 3RD

"I love you, Sweetie." I looked down at Gracelynn as we walked hand in hand out of the movie theater. A movie I'd promised to see during the school break, but I'd saved for *after* the 25th. So the girls, and one of Gab's friends, and I joined other parents and kids trying to find an outing on a brutally frigid afternoon.

Gracelynn didn't change the direction of her forward gaze as we walked through the theater lobby. I wondered if she'd even heard me. I got the sense she had, but I wouldn't know based on her gait. We continued through the doors out into the snow.

I say "I love you" to my kids often. Multiple times a day. And they sometimes keep moving ahead as if no air was expelled. It is not one of those things we say once as parents and then figure it's all good, we never need to cover the topic again. I want the words and the idea to wash over my children repeatedly, like waves. A rhythm of our life that they know they can count on. So I say it at random times, like walking out of a movie theater when I look down at my blonde-headed seven-year-old and have that twinge of "I wish I could freeze her in this spot forever." The words come out. When I am asking for forgiveness, "I love you" once again. When they've worked hard, been kind, or gotten into trouble and made a mess. In all circumstances, I tell them. And I do it over and over.

As I walked from the theater to the car, head bent toward the ground to keep the blowing snow out of my eyes, one little's hand in each of mine, dragging them through the cold, I wondered if that's the point of this Christmas. The over and over. The message on repeat. In all circumstances. Whether we acknowledge it or not, this message of "I love you," this love note of a Savior wrapped in swaddling clothes—more importantly, wrapped in skin—is to be the wave over us every year. "I love you." And again, "I love you." And a year later, when we've had a heck of a go at life and things aren't looking as we thought they would or should, "I love you" again.

Day 11: January 4th

I keep thinking about a song we sang at the Christmas Eve service. The words "my soul, my soul magnifies the Lord"[3] are straight from Scripture. Often referred to as "The Magnificat," this poem or song of Mary exclaiming her awe at the holiness of her circumstances expresses words we can echo, despite our less-than-magnificent circumstances.

I keep humming the song, the lyrics half whispered, half spoken, as I fold laundry, considering what it means for me. To *magnify* is to make bigger, more visible. I think of a magnifying glass that is held up to an object in order to see it better. Other translations of this verse read as "my soul glorifies the Lord."[4] I cannot make God bigger than he is. He is constant. But I can perhaps make him more visible. If he is indeed the very source of love, joy, peace, and hope, can I not be the visible personification of these elements to my little circle of influence?

> In the same way, let your light shine before others, so that they may see your good works and give glory to your Father in heaven. (Matthew 5:16 NRSV)

When I do a loving act, I am not only making God's character a wee bit more present on earth, I am also glorifying him, or saying how incredibly huge, indescribable, omnipotent he is. The words seem overused and insufficient to describe how my spirit responds to the knowledge of the holy. What I know is my soul resonates with this story. Though it be a bit ridiculous to many, a bit unbelievable from a rational place, it pierces my heart and I want more of it. My core hears the song it was made to listen to, this gospel, this good news of God on earth.

This message of "I love you," this love note of a Savior wrapped in swaddling clothes—more importantly, wrapped in skin—is to be the wave over us every year.

DAY 12: JANUARY 5TH

As this experiment comes to a close I go back to the book *The Liturgical Year*: "Christmas—the light that shone upon a manger—was also, the ancients knew, the light that led them on beyond it as well. If God is truly with us, has been manifested among us, companions us as we go, knows our pains and our hopes, then life is not a dark forest from which there is not exit. It is a darkness, however dark, that is always overcome by light."[5]

I read these words today and paused. I read them again. There is no denial here that life is difficult. There is no glossing over our actual lives with the Christmas spirit and a bit of eggnog and proclaiming it all magical. No, the entire purpose for this season is to remind us that Christmas changes the trajectory of our lives and the world.

When I do a loving act, I am not only making God's character a wee bit more present on earth, I am also glorifying him.

Chittister continues, "Christmas is larger than a baby in a manger. Christmas is the coming of a whole new world. More than that, it is what makes that world possible."[6] As I step out of Christmas and into the rest of the year, I remember that Christmas is not the beginning of the story—God existed before Jesus was born—but it is a crucial part. God entered his own creation in a humble, powerful move. He stepped onto earth in the way all of us have, that he might love us in the way no one else could.

What I Learned

There is a time in the season for quiet. For reflection and for stillness. From a practical standpoint, this is difficult to realize in the swirl of activities leading up to the 25th. But our church heritage almost knew we would have these modern Christmas problems and gave us this extended period to celebrate in a less-frenzied fashion.

This isn't the celebrating of the raucous party variety; we seem to reserve that for Advent. No this is more of an internal celebration, an absorption of what this story is all about. It is a message for our actual lives that not only acts as an annual reminder of God's larger story with humanity, but is also a balm that soothes our own souls and better prepares us to face the year ahead and do the good work in front of us.

He stepped onto earth in the way all of us have, that he might love us in the way no one else could.

In lots of ways this Christmastide looked like that of years past. I packed up boxes of decorations. I decided I need to eat better and exercise more in January. I felt an urge to clean out closets and organize life. The difference was, as I went through these familiar motions, I dwelled on the story. I soaked it in, remembering this is a message for my entire year, January through December. That my faith that hinges on the cross first needed a baby in the flesh. That Christmas isn't a race that ends on the 25th with recovery after, but a true season of relishing. Christmastide ensured the relishing.

Practices I'll Continue

- Schedule unscheduled days
- Make Boxing Day a day to send messages of love to those I miss
- Say yes as often as possible
- Be kind to my November self and pack up Christmas accordingly

QUESTIONS FOR REFLECTION

1. How has your soul been impacted this Christmas season?
2. What can you do to wrap up Christmas well from a practical standpoint?
3. How can you carry Christmas with you into the rest of the year?

Words for My Actual Christmas

My soul magnifies the Lord. (Luke 1:46 NRSV)

Conclusion

EMMANUEL, GOD WITH US

I knew something needed to be different. I couldn't do Christmas like I had in years past. And so an experiment to love my Christmas, right in the middle of my actual circumstances, was born. Just as I birth Christmas and all of its hoopla for my family every year, I created an intentional framework to examine how and why I do this holiday season in the first place.

The "Hows"

There were a few "hows" that stood out to me—those ways that we execute the crazy that is this season. Nothing surprising, more an affirmation of the things we suspect to be true which are confirmed when we try them. Here are the tactical approaches that made this year smoother than years past.

Planning Ahead

Scheduling, preparing ahead of time, pacing myself as I tackle the big events and the details all keep me from collapsing at the end of Christmas. A budget helps me stay on track. Even if I waiver a little in my spending, I'm closer to the goal than if I had no budget at all. And knowing what's ahead helps me communicate expectations to my people. They are both mentally and logistically prepared for how things are going to happen, which allows for a smoother execution of it all.

Recognizing Limitations

Darn it if I don't want to do it all, all of the time! And my human parameters get in the way, preventing me from proving my super-woman Christmas-orchestrating abilities. When I recognize where my limits lie, I can begin to prioritize my time, energy, money, and resources. I find places where I have to say no, whether in spending, time, or energy. I can also see potential openings for others to join me in this Christmas making, giving them an opportunity to enjoy the season while giving me a little help.

Making Space

Once I recognize my limitations, I can build in buffers of time so that I can actually participate in the fun, have some serene moments in this holy season and savor them! But I must be the one to make these intentional decisions. When left on its own, the crazy of Christmas will take over my life. Blocking out hours or even days for quiet, limiting activities or spending, even prioritizing eating and sleeping—all make space for my body, mind, and spirit to relish this season for a bit.

Stopping and Noticing

Once there is space in my day or my attention span, I am in charge of using it well. I must be the one to stop and say hello to the mail carrier, to listen to the lyrics of the Christmas carol, to read the Christmas story one more time. It is a discipline to step off the merry-go-round of busy and a second discipline to point my attention to the things of this season I want to relish. When I do this, I am overwhelmed with gratitude for the ways God has already given me much to celebrate.

Extending the Season

Just because Walmart is putting out Valentine's candy on Christmas Eve doesn't mean I have to move on. I can join with my brothers and sisters of the church who marinate in the anticipation of Jesus's arrival for four weeks and celebrate his coming for twelve days. This not only helps me pace the myriad of activities I want to jam into this magical window of time, it gives my heart room to dwell in the miracle of the story. There is more space, more room to stop and notice, more relishing if I move past the 25th and allow Christmas to dwell in my heart and my home for just a bit longer.

The "Whys"

All of these "hows" have to do with the executing of the season, the approaches I put into place. But what have I learned about the why? Why do we celebrate all of this in the first place?

The intentionality of the how did illuminate the why. As I carried out the experiment, I was reminded that this holiday becomes a circus because we are operating out of our longings. We long for memories and fun and happiness. We long for meaning and purpose. We know it must be hidden somewhere among the decorations and the fuss. And when I stopped and paid attention, this is what stood out to me about why we do all of this Christmas making in the first place.

Remember the Story

The story of Mary, Joseph, the angels and the shepherds, the innkeeper and the baby, is unlike any other stories of the season. *The Grinch That Stole Christmas* and Dickens's *A Christmas Carol* are told and retold this time of year because they are entertaining, but they are not from the pages of our holy text. This story of Baby Jesus is radically different, and it changed the course of history. It is a story our hearts need to hear. About Mary's willingness to be used by God, Joseph's radical obedience regardless of appearance, the shepherds' enthusiasm, and God's fulfillment of his promise to arrive as a baby. This story changes everything.

In All Circumstances

There is a reason we remember this part of God's story every year, no matter what is happening in our lives: because we need to hear it. We need to remember the "I love you" and "I came in the middle of the mess" in our own difficult circumstances and when life is going along just fine. In the easy and the difficult, we need to be reminded that God chose to enter the very space he created as a human to best express his love for us. That Christmas isn't about the mistletoe and tinsel and "the most wonderful time of the year." Though those things are fun, it's about the most loving God who came.

A Story for Everyone

No one is disqualified from this story's power. Everyone is welcome to come to the manger, peer in, and see what this baby is all about. When we peel back the layers of those desires of the season, of purpose and meaning, deep down I believe our longing lies in love. We have been created to be loved and that is why this story resonates with our spirits. God so loved the world he sent . . . a baby. From the working shepherds to the royal wise men, the message is the same. "I am bringing you good news of great joy for all the people,"[1] not for those of a certain gender, race, socioeconomic class, or education level. For all people of all times.

Christmas Permeates the Year

So this story sets the tone for the coming year. This intersection of the liturgical calendar with the annual calendar gives us a chance to enter the New Year with a fresh sense of God's love for us through Jesus. It can shape our thoughts, perspectives, attitudes, and even hopes if we let it. It can direct our relationships, work, finances, and callings. God so loved the world he sent . . . a baby. The head knowledge and the heart change can influence our daily life from the big to the small.

An experiment to love my actual Christmas not only changes my holiday from a practical and spiritual perspective, it ends up changing me. I leave this season renewed as I remember what I've already known about God. I've heard this story many times and am once again relearning its significance to the world and my life. I also leave this season enlightened, having learned new aspects of the characters, their stories, and how they butt up against my actual life with insight and clarity.

Christmas pushes toward Easter. We can't have the cross—the crux of our faith, Jesus sacrificed so all might live freely—unless we also have the manger. And the manger doesn't mean as much unless we see it in context of the cross and the resurrection. All of this can get lost in the Christmas concerts and velvet dresses and strung popcorn on the tree. From the perfect Christmas card to the perfect turkey dinner we are easily distracted by the business of Christmas making. The recalibration of our hearts must focus in on this story and see it in light of God's bigger story.

Loving this Christmas, relishing the season, is about both the how and the why. The executing and the understanding. The living and the believing. Emmanuel, God with us, for all of history and for today. For you and for me. For tomorrow and forever. Every year we have an opportunity to relish the story that changed everything. When that is our goal, our priorities get realigned and we make decisions accordingly.

Emmanuel, God with us. May Christmas be an annual reminder that he is here no matter our actual circumstances. This is a year to celebrate the good news within the context of our actual lives.

Making Your Actual Christmas Work

PRACTICAL TIPS AND STRATEGIES FOR YOUR HOLIDAY

Schedule

SAVING TIME FOR
WHAT'S MOST IMPORTANT

Scheduling Principles

On top of the crazy busy that our actual lives include—work, home, kids, sports, carpool, homework, doctors' appointments, grocery shopping, and a thousand other little details that fill up our days— we throw in the extras of the holidays. This can be parties (work, school, and family), concerts, pageants, tree cutting, gingerbread house making, caroling, service projects, decorating, card addressing, shopping, wrapping, baking, and on and on.

I would love to do all these fun Christmas extras, the operative word here being *fun*. Is it fun if I'm exhausted to the point of tears? If I'm running in and out of crowded stores every day tracking down sprinkles for the cookie decorating party, trying to prepare for the next great "memory making" activity? If I'm upset that my family isn't appreciating all of the hard work I've put into making this special memory a reality?

In a word, no. Not fun for me. And usually not fun for those around me who have to deal with the Christmas momzilla.

At some point we have to come to terms with our limit of twenty-four hours in every day. We simply cannot do it all. This, of course, points to expectations. Ours and others'. It also gets us to accept that we have limited time and energy. There is no perfect Christmas, no perfect executors of it, no one way to do things. We all must prioritize based on what's most important to us and our family.

The metaphor most helpful to me is the big rock principle. This common illustration is worth noting here as we choose from a large menu of possible time-consuming activities. It is this. Picture your finite time—in our case, the Christmas season—as a mason jar. Potential activities are represented by rocks that fill in the jar. In this case, we will assign activities with a higher priority a larger rock status. You must choose those big, important rocks and put them in the jar first. You can then pour in and fill around with smaller rocks, and even smaller gravel or sand after that. If you put those less important activities in the jar first, it will fill with sand and the important "big rocks" won't fit in.

I aim for three holiday-specific activities that I will include leading up to Christmas (one big thing per weekend during Advent). I put these on our schedule (aka in our jar) as soon as I can, often months in advance. These activities will vary from person to person, family to family. The traditions, special events, or surprises you really want to make happen are set on your calendar and the time is reserved.

The less important priorities can then fit in around my "big rocks." This is where self-control must enter the picture. Because it's easy, oh so easy, to say yes to just one more activity, and before we know it we are back on Team Exhausted. Make decisions regarding the smaller rocks with this question in mind: Will this energize or deplete me and those in my charge? Personality, age, and other commitments will feed into your answer. But this is your actual Christmas, and it's okay to take a pass on some things.

Extending the season also helps. We tend to act like crazy women up until December 25th and then collapse from exhaustion on the 26th. Yet we often have downtime in our schedules through the New Year holiday. This extension, known as Christmastide in the church liturgical calendar (or twelve days of Christmas), is built into our calendars to relish the season. To slow down and sit in the quiet of the knowledge that Jesus has come. We can simply move some of those memory-making activities and social obligations to that time when we are done shopping and wrapping and can simply enjoy.

See:
Christmastide,
page 83.

BUT MOM . . . WE ALWAYS

Evaluating Traditions

Traditions offer us markers. The very fact that we celebrate Christmas is a tradition, something we do annually. The memories we make by doing the same things with the same people help build meaning into the rhythm of the year and the season. But our options for memory making are often more plentiful than the time, energy, or budget our sanity can afford. Evaluating needs and desires from year to year can help us determine which traditions to prioritize.

The stress of "But we ALWAYS . . ." is real in my home. It doesn't matter if it's making Christmas cookies or cutting down the tree, in recent years I've put the kibosh on some cherished traditions because they weren't going to work for our family any longer. If you are going to love your actual Christmas, here is where expectations may need to be adjusted. What truly matters? What do you want to remember a year from now? Ten years from now? Will beginning or continuing a particular tradition help you get there?

Here are some questions to consider when deciding to keep or ditch a given tradition:

Who does it involve? Those around us can have strong feelings, often surprising to us as the Christmas orchestrators, about which traditions to keep and which to let go of. Traditions I thought would be important aren't. And activities I thought were a nice memory from years past are suddenly in the "tradition" category. Ask those around you what they want to keep. Also consider if a tradition is an opportunity to see extended family or a group of friends that you want to make a priority this season. Perhaps a tradition is worth maintaining because it builds time with important people into our busy schedules.

What is the opportunity cost? The laws of economics say scarce resources should be used to their maximum potential. So often you need to give up a good option in order take advantage of the best one. What are you giving up in order to say yes to this tradition? Does going to the live nativity keep you from going to your sister-in-law's wreath-making party? What will this activity cost you in time, money, and energy? What do you gain by continuing with the tradition, and what would you gain by letting it go? Will the nativity help you reach a larger goal of helping your children understand the Christmas story? Will there be relational fallout if you miss your sister-in-law's event? After the questions are asked and answered, is it still something you want to pursue?

Is it fun anymore? Maybe when your kids were younger going to stand in line to see Santa was magical and memorable and offered all kinds of photo ops . . . and maybe now not so much. Maybe it used to be fun to go to high tea with your friends, and now it feels like an obligation that you must fit into your budget and your schedule. Traditions, for the most part, are meant to be *fun*. If they've lost their zing, bless and release. Recognize they were good for a season, but you are not obligated to them for the next.

Does it need to be adjusted? Sometimes a tradition doesn't need to be thrown out altogether, it simply needs to be fine-tuned to meet your actual circumstances in a given year. A concert can go from evening to matinee to decrease cost. A party can go from dinner party to open house to adjust for kids' basketball schedules or to include a larger guest list. Decorating the tree can be taken over by older children, simply because they are capable. Adjusting a tradition keeps the celebration and the essence of the custom while recognizing that our contexts for Christmas have changed.

Do you just need to skip a year? Last year I didn't send Christmas cards. I just couldn't muster the strength to do them. It was the first time in eighteen years I hadn't. I knew I wasn't ending the tradition forever, but I also knew I might lose my marbles if I needed to track down missing addresses amid the chaos. This year I'm picking it back up. Did anyone die in the process? No. Do I regret it? Only a little. Can I do them this year even though I didn't last? Of course. Sometimes giving yourself the needed space to say "We'll try again next year" will be the difference between sanity and the Christmas meltdown.

Traditions are often the very things that make the Christmas season memorable. They can also be the extras that throw us into the exhausted, stressed-out category. Be flexible in how you approach them, asking key questions along the way, and you will surely love your Christmas a little more.

THE POWER OF NO THANK YOU

Limiting Commitments

Okay, this is where it gets hard. Where the rubber of priorities hits the road. The word *no* feels loaded to us sometimes. Because we are afraid we will hurt someone's feelings. Because we want to say yes. Because we are worried we will disappoint others. Once those big rocks are set, there is stronger clarity around what to say yes to, but also what to say no to. Here are some things I can tell you about *no*:

An invitation is just that. Most sane people understand your time is limited and that they are inviting you, not requiring you, to attend an event. A "no thank you," "not this year," or "I would have loved to, but maybe next year" are all acceptable responses to an invitation.

Delivery makes a difference. As you deliver the "no thank you," assume a posture of gratitude for being included. "Thank you for inviting us; we can't make it this time." Affirm that time is the constraint, not the event itself (if that truly is the case—we don't want to make up stories just to make someone feel better). "I've wanted to see that movie too. We just can't fit it in during this Christmas month." Make plans to be together post-Christmas. "How about a January sledding date instead?" This affirms the importance of the relationship and conveys that the limitation is time, not desire to be together.

You are not obligated to make everyone happy. In some ways this goes against all things Christmas frenzy, doesn't it? But truly, it is not your job in the world to please everyone. You don't need to apologize for being a human constrained by space and time. Will some people be unhappy when you say no? Yes. Does that make you a mean person? Not if you delivered the message with a kind spirit (see above). We do have to balance this with our choice to sacrificially love by making someone else's priorities our own. When we make that choice, we must remember we are doing it out of a spirit of love, not arm-twisting, and therefore act accordingly. ✦

See: Bringing Families Together, page 121.

Finances

TAKING IT TO THE BANK

Saving Money during Christmas

When we think of Christmas we often think price tags. On gifts, obviously, but on other costs too: travel, special meals, Christmas cards, teacher gifts, service provider gifts, decorations, and tickets to special shows. The cost of the season can quickly add up. But we don't have to let it get out of control.

Jesus didn't come to earth in order that we might overspend every December and have terrible arguments about the holiday bills. He came that we might have life. Let's figure out what we can afford and live within those parameters.

This seems obvious, but creating a budget is the crucial step to fighting overspending that most often gets ignored. Frequently because we don't know where to begin. Let me suggest you start with the end in mind. Ask yourself, and your spouse, what amount on the January credit card bill will make you happy? And if happy seems a bit out of reach, what can you live with? Truly, what can your family absorb as far as spending? Take that number and work backwards.

Here are a few things to remember when creating your budget:

- If you are married and share the money you will be spending, you must agree on a seasonal maximum. If you can't agree, defer to the lesser bottom line between the two of you.

- Do not consider the budgets of those around you. This may be very difficult, but to love your actual Christmas, you must embrace your actual budget. What *your* family can afford. Comparison in any area is a joy killer.

- Do an inventory of spending. Write down everything you will want to spend money on over the season that is above and beyond what is typically in your budget. Categories could include, but are not limited to:

    Gifts for those in your home

    Gifts for those at work

    Gifts for extended family

    Gifts for the helpers (teachers, pastors, postal workers)

    Party costs (those you host and those you attend)

    Special meals (don't forget cookies)

    Decorations (including a tree if you buy one every year)

    Charitable giving / Christmas church offerings

    Travel (including additional gas for special events)

    Christmas cards (don't forget postage)

    Tickets for pageants, concerts, shows, etc.

    Clothes! (Christmas jammies and Santa pictures, anyone?)

    Oh yeah, Santa pictures

This is a sampling of category ideas, but you may have others you want to add, like a new punch bowl for Uncle Arnold's annual eggnog contest. You know your actual life and what will come around this year.

Now that you've started to feel your breath shorten and a full-on panic attack is welling up, tell yourself this is possible, you can make a plan. Begin to divvy up your bottom-line budget number among these items. And eliminate where you can (or where you have to).

REDUCE, REUSE, RECYCLE

Gift Giving on a Budget

If the budget is tight, as in pinching pennies, Christmas can feel beyond stressful. There are ways to save some money in the gift-giving area no matter what the bottom-line budget number. Not every strategy will work for everyone, but here are a few to get ideas going.

Simply eliminate. Just because you have given your neighbor a gift every year doesn't mean you've committed to it forever. Oh, beware of the things that happen once and can unintentionally become "traditions." The office party. The in-laws' gift exchange. Where can you step away for a year? It can be hard, even embarrassing, to remove yourself from a group effort, but consider why you are participating. If it is out of pride, it may deserve to make the cut.

Three gifts. Based on the story of Jesus being visited by the magi or three wise men, each bearing a gift, a limit of three gifts per child (or family member) can keep you from buying "just one more thing." It makes us prioritize how we want to spend our money, and in the end it eliminates clutter too. I tell my children, "If it was good enough for Baby Jesus, it's good enough for you."

Something you want. Something you need. Something to wear. Something to read. Rather than just limiting the number of gifts each family member receives, this little rhyme helps diversify the gift giving too. This has been my personal favorite the last few years, especially with older kids. It helps set their expectations and promises both fun and practical items under the tree. (A twist if you feel like your child has everything he "needs": offer an experience with a parent or sibling in its place.)

Give to one in a group. The gift exchange is a tradition for many—often a way to celebrate a group without giving to every member. Consider converting a group that has traditionally exchanged gifts to a gift exchange in which names are selected and one person gives to only one other member of the group. This could be neighbors, your teammates at work, the adults in your extended family, or even cousins. Buying for one person rather than twelve obviously can make an impact on your budget. A structure like this can offer other guidelines like spending limits (yay!) or a gift theme.

New to them. If the first four points were about Reduce, this is about Reuse and Recycle. Figure out ways to swap items you already have with others who are looking to do the same. The younger your children are, the easier this is to do. Hold a toy swap, book swap, or clothing swap where everyone brings items in good condition that they would like to trade for something else. And when in doubt, hit the thrift stores! Your three-year-old is never going to know he wasn't the first to play with that $3 fire engine.

Shop all year. If you are reading this in July, you can benefit from this approach. Have a corner of a closet or a bag that is your spot for clearance items you discover all year long. This allows you to maximize sale prices and spread your spending over a number of months. Great for stocking stuffers, teacher gifts, and that treat for the mail carrier.

Avoid temptation. Don't go to the mall or the home-based shopping party. Just don't. Throw catalogs away. Consolidate your shopping into one trip or one two-hour chunk online with a predetermined list. Have your budget at the forefront of your mind, and stick to what you want to give, not to what is screaming to you from that Facebook ad in your sidebar.

As far as expectations for the Christmas season go, gift giving is one area where our reality may not be able to meet our desires.

With a little creativity, and perhaps some honest reflection, you can come up with a gift-giving list that will honor the recipients while honoring your checking account. Peeling back the reasons we give gifts in the first place, we find it's to show love to those around us. To let people know we see and value them. This has nothing to do with how much we spend, but the thoughtfulness of the items we give.

LOOKING FOR THE CHEAP

Other Savings Tips

No question, gifts are the biggest source of budget stress during the holidays, but there are other hidden costs of Christmas. Here are a few ways to watch your budget beyond gift giving.

Find the free fun. Tree lighting ceremonies, outdoor or church-based concerts, Santa at the mall (if you aren't obligated to purchase a photo package). Get holiday books from the library to add some snuggle reading time in the evenings. Some might even like to go Christmas caroling (though I am not one of them, but I am willing to make cocoa for those who do). Memories don't have to cost money. Fun can be free.

See: Reduce, Reuse, Recycle, page 116.

Decorate with found objects. Cut out paper snow-flakes, string popcorn, spray-paint pinecones or broken tree branches. All things you can use to decorate your table, mantel, or tree on the cheap. My mom still has a set of wooden ornaments she found in our neighbor's trash when I was little. More than thirty years later they are still beautiful.

Beware of the homemade. You've likely seen that meme that says, "I could have bought it for $5 or made it for $68.93 in supplies." That scrapbook that requires a special die-cut machine. The cutting board that requires a new table saw. You get the idea. If you need to make a capital investment to do a project, it often isn't less expensive to make it yourself. Homemade can be thoughtful and special, but if the goal is saving money, run the numbers first.

(Hint: Typically the more of a single item you make, the lower the cost per item. So making gifts in bulk helps with costs.)

Use your kitchen: aka cook. As opposed to homemade gifts, homemade food is almost always significantly less expensive. Busy schedules can make eating on the run the fallback. Restaurant prices, even fast food, can quickly add up. As you begin the season, double quantities as you prepare dinners and freeze half so you can have some quick meals on the ready at home to prevent tempting last-minute eating out. Prepared foods at the grocery store (think veggie trays) also cost more. So as you add that work party to your calendar, set aside time to shop and prepare your assigned appetizer at home. Besides, the food will likely taste better too.

Relationships

BRINGING FAMILIES TOGETHER

Navigating Extended Family Relationships

Not every person struggles with family dynamics during the holiday season. However, it is common to feel the pressure of expectations of extended family, both from our family of origin and the family we married into, at a time of year when we are already pulled thin and exhausted. When I surveyed women about their holiday stress, managing extended family dynamics was one of their biggest barriers to loving their actual Christmas.

Many of us struggle with the spoken and unspoken expectations of those beyond our immediate circle—pressure to do certain things or to show up in certain places. Every family's dynamics are unique. They are centered on family roles, traditions, centers of power, and larger hopes. As people grow up, move out, and make decisions for themselves, it's hard on those left behind. And then babies come and new families are made and well . . . it can feel tricky at minimum.

Because every family is different, there is not a one-size-fits-all family management strategy, but here are a few principles that may help when trying to figure out how to respond to the stressors of family dynamics:

Honor both sides. If you are married, you are combining two sets of Christmas traditions—the "how we've always done its" and, dare I say, "right ways" of doing the holiday. You may not be the only one who has hopes for how the season will look (okay, there's a stating of the obvious). And if you have children, you are passing these ideas and traditions down. Don't automatically pull the Christmas orchestrator trump card on your husband . . . or his family. Your traditions should reflect both sides. If they are leaning a little heavy your way, adjust. If you feel like you are giving up too much, be clear about the changes you would like to see while keeping in mind the next point.

Be kind. Always. That's right, kindness is a goal. If you need to miss an event or ask family to pare down on the gift giving for your kids, say it in the kindest way you can muster. You may know the news is going to be disappointing to the recipient, you may even know it's not going to be well received, but it will be received better if you are kind in the delivery and express gratitude, acknowledging the family member's good motives when possible. The goal is to communicate that the relationship matters, even as you work out the details.

Table larger issues. If it feels like the holiday battles are microcosms of bigger battles (i.e., communication styles, expectations, dysfunctional behaviors), this may not be the place or time to get into those. Deal with the holiday and its unique responsibilities and challenges apart from the larger issues. And make a commitment to yourself, and perhaps your spouse, that you will develop a plan to address the larger dynamics when appropriate. This isn't about pretending problems away. It's about figuring out how to make your holiday work for you without creating World War III.

See: Believing the Best in Others, page 124.

Christmas can bring out the best and worst of extended family dynamics. If the goal is to love your actual Christmas, find a way to live in your family that honors the people around you while making space for your fun and peace. If little eyes are watching, we must remember we are modeling what it means to be in relationships. How we treat our extended family holds many lessons for them about what family and friendship look like.

BELIEVING THE BEST IN OTHERS

Taking a Posture of Grace

We live life as imperfect people, bumping up against other imperfect people. This relationship stuff is rarely neat and tidy. The world is a rough place, and when possible we need to cut each other a break, to believe the best in each other and for each other.

In a time of year when we are often in close proximity with people, either by choice or forced reunion, we may easily fall into old patterns. Here's what I know: we can't control how others behave, but we can always control how we behave. It may not take long for your brother to say something that takes you right back to your childhood and you hear the words "He always . . ." or "He never . . ." start to run through your head. Your fuse will be longer if you start the reconnection choosing to believe the best in him.

If it feels hard to make that mental adjustment of believing the best in someone, try these tricks:

- Make a list of everything you appreciate about that person. Get creative. If nothing else, the ridiculous items on the list will make you laugh.
- Consider the concerns the other person is bringing into the holiday season. This will help you remember the stress they are currently carrying and grow your empathy.
- Recruit a team to help you love others well. Ask your husband (or your sister or your mom, anyone who can read you) to

give you a signal when you are starting to default into old patterns. Code phrases like "Marcie just texted me" can clue you to reel it in.

- Pray for the other person. God has a way of making that heart adjustment on our behalf when we ask him to.

- Don't expect perfection from someone who can't offer it. Remember the imperfect person formula that's playing out? Unrealistic expectations of others (and ourselves) need to be squashed.

- Try to have fun together. This can remind us about what we love, even like, about the person in front of us.

Sometimes it's just a mental recalibration, a choosing to believe the best in someone, that makes a world of difference in how holiday gatherings go down. And when it all fails, offer grace. What? You mean when she's rude to me? When he doesn't respect my wishes? When they go around me? Yes. Even then.

That baby in the manger who we celebrate this time of year is love personified. He is the Prince of Peace, the Reconciler, the definition of taking on more than his fair share of blame. We can celebrate him right here in the midst of our actual families by offering our families unmerited favor . . . otherwise known as *grace*. Rather than fighting back, grasping for what is "rightfully yours," remember that the grace offered you on the cross was undeserved, unmerited favor. When we practice this grace offering, we begin to change our perspective, our thoughts, and our attitudes. So we can, you know, love our actual Christmas.

STEWARDING THE STORY

Kids and the Christmas Story

Christmas and kids were made for each other. The main attraction in the story is a baby surrounded by animals, after all. It's like God wrote this chapter with a younger audience in mind.

No different than us, the children in our care need to hear and experience the story over and over. We are meant to steward this tale, to hold it for our generation and pass it down to the next so they can in turn pass it down someday. We know this miracle happened because there have been people of every generation since who have guarded and retold it. Now is our time to tell and retell so our children will absorb it into the fibers of their hearts. Here are a few ways to present these characters to our kids:

It is a story! Use books. Illustrated picture books. Board books. Lift-the-flap books. It doesn't matter, just read them—a book a night (or before naps). Go to thrift stores and build your stock that you pack away and bring back out every year with your Christmas decorations. Go to the library and raid their seasonal collection. We all know reading to and with kids is good for them in all kinds of ways. Why not read them stories that capture their imagination around this beautiful truth we are collectively celebrating?

Be tactile. Not every child learns by listening. Give kids tools to build with and touch. Make a stable with blankets. Have nativity sets they can play with and move around (and don't be surprised to find Joseph in the fridge or baby Jesus in the bathroom sink). Use

Play-Doh to make a manger or a star in the sky. God needed to come in an incarnational way with skin and bones that could touch and hug. No surprise many of us need to touch and feel details of the story for it to become more real.

Act it out. Nothing helps children absorb the story more than playing it out. Whether holding figurines from a nativity set or holding a baby doll, kids can take on the parts of the various characters. What did they say? Do? Feel? How did the others respond? As children consider what it felt like to journey on a donkey (and older kids make great donkeys, by the way) or to have an angel appear, the realities of the characters' experiences begin to sink in.

Sing the story. Christmas carols are a beautiful tradition that capture a small part of the larger story and focus in on it. Play "Little Drummer Boy" and ask kids what their gift to Jesus can be. Play "Away in a Manger" or "Silent Night" while your children lie with their eyes closed picturing the manger and the baby. Have a dance party to "Joy to the World" and remember that this is a birthday celebration we hold every year for God himself. Music speaks to our hearts and the lyrics of traditional carols help put the story on our lips.

Repeat. Repeat. Repeat. I've heard you must hear a word seven times in a new language before you remember it. It takes thirty days to build a habit. So no surprise, it takes repetition to remember and absorb a story. We need it and our children need it. And here's the benefit for us: when we repeat the story in these different ways for our kids' sakes, we are repeating it for our own hearts too.

Logistics

WHY ARE WE DOING THIS AGAIN?

Party Hosting Basics

From class parties to dinner parties, Christmas is full of extra festivities. If you are the planning person, you can put some tricks in place to help guests have a memorable time while maximizing efforts. You don't want to end the party season depleted by executing the details, but energized by the relationships that are strengthened by a shared time together. Here are a few tips on making your Christmas party one that is merry and bright:

Decide on the purpose. No matter the size, five or fifty, a party is meant for a group of people to get together to celebrate something. During the holidays a gathering can also act as an end-of-year marker. The party's purpose could be to applaud a year of projects completed, to offer a social time of fun and holiday spirit together, to continue a group tradition that has bonded members over the years, or simply to rejoice in friendship and the holy feast. Decide what you want guests to experience, how you want them to feel when leaving the party, and many of the planning details will fall into place.

Help guests mix. Have ways that move conversations past the superficial or awkward and into new and different topics. Since a party is meant to be a group experience, help people experience the group in a positive way and get natural conversations flowing by helping them make connections about work, interests, parenting, or anything else that will help jump-start conversations. Include an activity: a game, a performance, a hands-on craft, something to focus the room's attention on, a single pursuit to unify those who are together. It gives guests some direction and also provides a party flow leading up to and winding down from the "main thing."

Share the workload. There are no awards shows for Christmas party throwing. No prizes for "Best Able to Pull It Off Alone." Ask guests to bring food or help with decorations, invitations, setting up, or cleaning up. Everyone benefits from a party, and everyone is usually willing to chip in to make it happen. (If they aren't, just nominate them Scrooge for the season and move on to more willing folks.) Unless party planning and executing is your most favorite thing in the whole world, share the work this season when there are so many additional stresses on your calendar and energy.

Add the special. This gets to your purpose. Do you want guests to feel celebrated when they leave? Have a handwritten note of appreciation for each. Do you want to introduce invitees to one another? Create assigned seats for a meal, intentionally placing people together. Do you want the group to feel they've had a Christmas celebration? Make sure the music and decorations transform a classroom, office boardroom, or family room into something different than the typical. If you've recruited your team to share the workload, you should have enough space and energy to add the special touches that take a bit more effort and make the party memorable (in a good way).

WE STILL HAVE TO EAT

Decisions around Food Prep

Christmas brings with it special food. Meals and parties and traditions that can leave us over budget, overweight, and overstressed as we stay up past midnight rolling out our grandmother's cinnamon rolls and then eat three the next morning.

So what's a cook supposed to do with all of the extra food duties and expectations around the Christmas season?

Do what is fun. Make cookies with your kids. *If it is fun.* Offer to bring your famous artichoke dip to the office party. *If it is fun.* Host a dinner party for your apartment building. *You got it: if it is fun.* This is an area where stress can be eliminated by simply not volunteering. The special touches in the food arena can help set meals apart as something different, but don't let the different be that the cook is banging the pots and pans in the kitchen because she resents the extra work.

Do what is meaningful. If you have a cultural dish or a family recipe that you make every year, make that a priority. Tamales for Christmas Eve dinner are a lot of work, but if you are remembering your people as you make them, there is other value there. Holding a tradition that has been passed down can offer lots of significance to you and those you are teaching (such as children in your midst). This is your time to hold that tradition and subsequently pass it on down.

Do what is budget friendly. Special dishes often require special (aka expensive) ingredients. If your budget can't handle the extra cost, pass on making a particular dish. Christmas meals and appetizers can be delicious without being expensive. Your actual budget helps determine what you can and can't sign up for on the group potluck. That's okay. Someone needs to bring the bread. This year it can be you.

Do what is possible, outsource when possible. On the flip side, if your budget has some wiggle room, splurge in this area. If those traditional tamales can be made by the restaurant down the street and that is all the same to your family, then go ahead and give someone else some Christmas work by buying from them. The same is true for the office party sandwiches and the gluten-free snacks for the class social. Involve others in the food prep. Make that party a potluck or have everyone chip in to order out. Whether volunteer or paid help, you are one person. Do what only you can do.

Do what you can ahead of time. Can the ham be prepped in the morning? The mashed potatoes made early? The vegetables chopped for the veggie tray the night before? How about making some cookies and freezing them for next week's party? What can be done today will help tomorrow when there might not be the same window of time for the kitchen. Food consumption times can be busy, with lots of people we want to spend time with. Maximize togetherness by doing as much chopping, cooking, and freezing as you can do ahead. Because you don't want to be in the kitchen missing the very party you're hosting.

Acknowledgments

This book is evidence that Christmas miracles still happen. Finishing a book during the Christmas season with four children at home, after a most difficult fall, felt nearly impossible. Yet God was gracious and so were my people in helping to make it work.

First, I must thank the writing team that pushed this forward. My agent Teresa Evenson, and Baker Books ladies, Rebekah Guzman and Eileen Hanson, understood that women feel the crazy at Christmas. Thank you for advocating for this message of slowing down. Early readers Annie Rim, Paula Spratt, and Katie Estrada, I appreciated your real mom takes on the whole idea. To my mother-in-law/writing coach, Carol Kuykendall, thank you for spending days in the words and pointing out where I needed more. And to Nicci Jordan Hubert, your expertise in the editing department fine-tuned my voice. This wouldn't be the book it is without all of you.

To my sister cheerleaders here at home, and through The Open Door Sisterhood, you gave me pep talks and offered prayers on my behalf, so the miracle of getting it done could unfold. You gave me strength on days when I was doubtful this would happen because of the actual life swirling around. To my fellow co-conspirator on so many things, Krista Gilbert, thank you for your extra dose of sisterhood. #powertothesisterhood

And to the A-Team of my actual life that gave me space to work and cheered me on so I could hide away and write a few pages at a time, I owe the biggest thanks. To my mom, thank you for school pickups and childcare and letting me process my grief by typing out my words while you were processing your own profound loss. To Carol, thank you for dinners for my family and vacation adventures with kids so I could focus for chunks of time on this. To my girls, thank you for understanding that this work is part of who I am and therefore takes up part of my days. And for Derek, thank you for the dinner making, flexing, and understanding involved in making this hodgepodge schedule work.

To God be the glory. His story is one worth telling over and over. Thank you, readers, for taking it in with me. For God so loved the world . . . he sent a baby. May we all remember this with joy and anticipation every year. Thank you, Lord, for this story worth telling and living.

Notes

Introduction

1. See Gary Chapman, *The Five Love Languages: The Secret to Love That Lasts* (Chicago: Northfield, 2015).

2. Alexandra Kuykendall, *Loving My Actual Life: An Experiment in Relishing What's Right in Front of Me* (Grand Rapids: Baker, 2016).

3. Joan Chittister, *The Liturgical Year: The Spiraling Adventure of the Spiritual Life* (Nashville: Thomas Nelson, 2009), 40.

Advent Week 1: Hope

1. Eugene H. Peterson, *The Message Remix: The Bible in Contemporary Language* (Colorado Springs: NavPress, 2003), Luke 2.

2. Luke 1:38.

3. http://www.metrolyrics.com/o-holy-night-lyrics-christmas-carols.html.

Advent Week 2: Love

1. *Merriam-Webster's Collegiate Dictionary*, 11th ed., s.v. "love."

2. Larry Crabb, *A Different Kind of Happiness: Discovering the Joy That Comes from Sacrificial Love* (Grand Rapids: Baker Books, 2016), 85.

Advent Week 3: Joy

1. http://www.lyricsmode.com/lyrics/c/christmas_songs/joy_to_the_world.html.

2. John 19:30.

3. Karen Ehman, *Listen, Love, Repeat: Other-Centered Living in a Self-Centered World* (Grand Rapids: Zondervan, 2016), 142.

4. John 16:21.

5. John 16:22.

Advent Week 4: Peace

1. Isaiah 9:6.

2. Eugene Cho, Facebook post, December 16, 2016, https://www.facebook.com/eugenecho/?fref=ts.

3. Corey Francis Parks, Medium.com, December 21, 2016, https://medium.com/@corriefrancis/the-individual-grain-7f8b05bc1751#.z2aqh34nn.

Christmastide

1. Matthew Diebel, "What You Need to Know about Boxing Day," *USA Today*, December 26, 2015.

2. The Customs of Christmastide, http://holytrinitygerman.org/xmascustoms.html#xmascustoms.

3. See Luke 1:46 NRSV.

4. Luke 1:46.

5. Chittister, *Liturgical Year*, 90.

6. Ibid., 94.

Conclusion

1. Luke 2:10 NRSV.

Alexandra Kuykendall spends her days driving to multiple schools, figuring out what to feed her people, and searching for a better solution to the laundry dilemma. Author of *Loving My Actual Life: An Experiment in Relishing What's Right in Front of Me* and *The Artist's Daughter: A Memoir*, Alex is cohostess of *The Open Door Sisterhood* podcast. A trusted voice in mothering circles, Alex speaks to women around the world about issues of parenting, faith, and identity. She lives in the shadows of downtown Denver with her husband, Derek, and their four daughters. You can connect with her at AlexandraKuykendall.com.

Inspiration for your everyday

In this entertaining and insightful book, Alexandra Kuykendall chronicles her nine-month experiment to rekindle her love of her ordinary, actual life. After wiping her calendar as clean as a mother of four can, Kuykendall focuses on one aspect of her life each month, searching for ways to more fully enjoy her current season. With humor, poignancy, and plenty of personal stories, she shows how a few small changes can make this crazy-busy life one of holy contentment.

CONNECT WITH

ALEXANDRAKUYKENDALL.COM

Alex_Kuykendall

AlexandraKuykendall.Author

Alexandra Kuykendall

LIKE THIS BOOK?

Consider sharing it with others!

- Share or mention the book on your social media platforms. Use the hashtag **#LovingMyActualChristmas.**

- Write a book review on your blog or on a retailer site.

- Pick up a copy for friends, family, or strangers— anyone who you think would enjoy and be challenged by its message!

- Share this message on Instagram, Twitter, or Facebook: **I loved #LovingMyActualChristmas by @Alex_Kuykendall // @ReadBakerBooks**

- Recommend this book for your church, workplace, book club, or class.

- Invite Alex to speak at your event.

- Follow Baker Books on social media and tell us what you like.

 Facebook.com/ReadBakerBooks

 @ReadBakerBooks